To Mark—

Tory, but more contented than Sibthorp ever was!

Sir Benjamin Stone 1838-1914: Photographer, Traveller and Politician

Stephen Roberts

Best—

Stephen Roberts

16 June 2014

Published by the Author under his imprint *Birmingham Biographics*

Printed by CreateSpace

ISBN-13: 978-1499265521

ISBN-10: 1499265522

THE LIBRARY OF BIRMINGHAM

For My Mother

Contents

Acknowledgements

𝕴 have been interested in Sir Benjamin Stone for more than three decades. I first wrote about him in 1979-85, producing first of all - under the rigorous supervision of John Bourne at the University of Birmingham - an undergraduate dissertation on his political career and soon after an unpublished biographical study deposited with Birmingham Public Libraries and two essays in a now-defunct scholarly journal. During those years I was very fortunate to come into contact with Stone's grand daughters Betty Cooper and Jane Brooker. They treated me with immense kindness, providing me with warm hospitality at their homes in, respectively, rural Shropshire and Highgate, London.

It was early one morning in spring 2013 that I was unexpectedly seized by a determination to write the biography of Stone that I had, over the years, occasionally contemplated doing. In truth I had never quite escaped Stone: whenever I visited Local Studies in the former Birmingham Central Library, the first thing I saw was his huge portrait gazing down at me. It seemed that, if I was ever going to tell his story, it had to be in 2014, the centenary of his death. I have once again benefited from the interest and encouragement of the Stone family. Stone's great-grandson Roger entertained me with some splendid anecdotes over lunch, and kindly gave me permission to quote from material I had examined in 1979 at the home of Jane Brooker. Jane O'Dell, the great-great niece of Stone's wife, shared with me letters in her possession, and enthusiastically welcomed the news of a biography.

I owe a very real debt to Peter James of the Library of Birmingham. Over the years we have had many conversations about Stone, and, during the writing of this book, he has given me much assistance. He has patiently answered numerous queries, read part of the book and has helped me to select the photographs which appear in it. These photographs are reproduced by permission of the Library of Birmingham. My thanks are also due to the staff of the Wolfson Centre for Archival Research at the Library of Birmingham, who have regularly retrieved - sometimes not without much patient searching - material for me. At Sutton Coldfield Library Ariadne Plant was particularly helpful. Roger Lea of the Sutton Coldfield Local History Research Group has kindly answered a number of queries. The cartoon from the *Dart* which features on the cover of this book is reproduced by permission of the Birmingham and Midland Institute.

I am grateful to Ian Cawood for his interesting comments on the fourth chapter. A word of thanks is also due to Peter Marsh, author of a magisterial biography of Joseph Chamberlain and with whom I have, over several meals, discussed both Joe and Stone to my considerable profit.

I wish to record my gratitude to the Trustees of the Sutton Coldfield Charitable Trust for their financial support. In particular I wish to thank Ernie Murray for putting forward my case to the Trustees and David Owen for his enthusiasm and interest. For their support and practical assistance during the publication process I am indebted to Kate Pool of the Society of Authors and Richard Brown.

This book is dedicated to my mother. Without her concern that I should receive a good education – oh, those mock 11+ examination papers during the summer holidays! – I would not have been able to spend my adult life engaged in the enjoyable and rewarding pleasure of writing books.

Preface

Sir Benjamin Stone lived a full life, and was certainly a more contented man than his restless Birmingham contemporary Joseph Chamberlain. Elected to Parliament in 1895, Stone would have been an undistinguished backbencher had it not been for his camera. On the terrace of the House of Commons he lined up his fellow-MPs and various interesting visitors to have their pictures taken. Dubbed 'Sir Snapshot' by the press, he became in these years the most well-known amateur photographer in the country. Stone was an intrepid traveller too, embarking – equipped, of course, with his camera – on a voyage around the world in 1891 and a journey of almost one thousand miles up the Amazon in 1893. He was also an insatiable collector, particularly of botanical and geological specimens. A shrewd businessman, with investments in glass and paper manufacture and house-building and quarrying, Stone had no difficulty in finding the funds for all of these interests. A genial and curious man, he formed warm friendships with like-minded men, and, at The Grange, his home in Erdington, Birmingham, presided over a family of six children. Stone was also a Tory politician. He doggedly promoted the Tory cause in Liberal-dominated Birmingham in the 1870s and early 1880s, and, after the Liberal rupture over Irish Home Rule in 1886, became an equally-determined supporter of the new Unionist alliance.

Drawing on newspapers and his own extensive personal papers, this is the first biography of Sir Benjamin Stone to be written. It is published to mark the centenary of his death.

1 Early Years

Iohn Benjamin Stone was born into a community on the cusp of change. In Duddeston, on the east side of Birmingham, there were metal-rolling mills and workshops but there were also green fields - though soon these were to be covered by cheap housing. East Birmingham was an area he was to get to know well – where he was to live, where he was to make his money and where he was to solicit the votes of working men. Though he was extremely well-travelled, Stone was not a man to uproot himself: he died only a few miles from where he was born. The house where he was born, on 9 February 1838, in Great Brook Street was only a short distance from the glass house in Dartmouth Street where his father had just been promoted from clerk to manager.

Benjamin Stone, thirty-five years old and from the Black Country, had married Rebecca Matthews in March 1836 after the death the previous year of his first wife Catherine Baker, and already had three children, Joseph, James and Catherine. With the arrival of three more children in four years, Benjamin and two daughters Rebecca in 1839 and Clara two years later, the family moved to a larger house in Lupin Street in Duddeston. They were always able to employ a servant, in 1841 sixteen year old Margaret Jones. Each morning as he grew up, Stone watched his father leave the house for the short walk to the glass house, soon to be joined by his half-brother, James, who was nine years older than him. James worked as a clerk, but also took responsibility for organising evening classes for the employees. Stone always knew that he would one day join them both.

It seems likely that Stone's early education took place at a school run by the Church of England. Certainly his father was a prominent member of the local Anglican congregation, and Stone secured a place at King Edward's School in New Street in 1850 after being proposed by one of the clergymen who served on the governing body. His nomination as a day boy meant that his father paid no fees, and, for two years, Stone settled into his studies. In charge was the Revd. E. H. Gifford, like most of the headmasters of King Edward's regarded as a brilliant scholar. If he did not particularly distinguish himself, Stone certainly held his own: 'very satisfactory', read his report of December 1850, 'he is going on well

1

and promises fairly'. [1] His only notable achievement was a prize for drawing, a talent which his father sought to encourage by briefly enrolling him after he left school at the School of Design. Stone was certainly proving himself an inquisitive boy. It was at this time that he began to develop his life-long passion for collecting. With his net and small bottle of laudanum, Stone went out collecting butterflies in the soon-to-disappear open spaces of Nechells, which he then mounted. Such was his interest that he subscribed to, and even wrote to, the entomologist magazine, the *Substitute*. Soon Stone was extending his passion for collecting with the purchase of his first geological specimens.

Like many of the manufacturing businesses in Birmingham, George Bacchus & Sons' Union Glassworks sought to get ahead of competitors by pioneering new techniques. In the 1830s, the firm became the first to produce pressed glass by using a plunger to force molten glass into a plain or patterned mould. The business specialized in producing fine glassware for the table. Such was reputation of Bacchus & Sons that Prince Albert paid a visit when he undertook a tour of several factories in Birmingham in November 1843. This royal look-around 'caused a great influx of visitors to the factory for several years and it was inspected by most of the celebrities of the time'. With the death of George Bacchus, his sons took charge and the firm continued to flourish, becoming especially well known for beautifully-designed paperweights. [2] Stone joined his father and half-brother as a clerk at the firm in 1852, and was soon saving money with one of the town's building societies. The following year James married Elizabeth Benton, leaving the family home and shortly afterwards becoming involved in his father-in-law's brass house.

In June 1860, Stone, his father and Frederick Fawdry, the son of a corn dealer who had married his half-sister Catherine, raised

---

[1] Library of Birmingham, Sir J. B. Stone Invitation Cards, Vol. 1.

[2] Library of Birmingham, Letters, Accounts, Documents etc. relating to the Union Glassworks. The firm was established in 1817 and was so named because 'if we all three…let a Union of Temper be preserved at all times, this will produce a happy and profitable Union': George Bacchus to George Green, 6 November 1817. Library of Birmingham, Sir J. B. Stone Newspaper Cuttings, Vol. 27, *Birmingham Daily Gazette*, 1 October 1849, for a description of the products of Bacchus & Sons.

the cash to buy out the Bacchus family. Keen to develop a business which had been embroiled in a bitter region-wide dispute over wage rates the previous year, they advertised immediately for 'a few steady hands, good workmen'. A loss of £283 in the first year was soon turned round into a steady profit which was maintained for seventeen years. The firm did particularly well in the 1860s, making annual profits of in excess of £2,000 and, in 1864, a record profit of £3,572. In newspaper advertisements the business emphasised its range – from glassware with 'the newest styles of patterns and designs' to that 'of the cheapest descriptions'. Their products were also put on show, for example, at the Birmingham Cattle and Poultry Exhibition in December 1862 which, over several days, admitted many thousands of people. [3]

Stone, Fawdry, Stone was a sizeable enterprise, employing, in 1861, eighty men, seventeen boys and five women, figures which had not changed significantly a decade later. One glassblower, Benjamin Cooke, revealed in 1864 that he was earning 21s a week with an additional 5s for overtime. From their pay the workers, like many of those in the factories of Birmingham, contributed to charitable causes – for example, they collected £1.1s and £1.12s respectively in 1861-1862 to relieve distress in Birmingham and in Lancashire. In March 1863, there was entertainment to mark the marriage of Prince Albert Edward; but glass houses were unpleasant places to work.[4] One young man, Stephen Bevan, reported in 1865:

The putty affects the nerves very much when it gets in and makes you feel very low. It also makes you sick, 'stakes up' the chest and makes the bowels costive ... When I am puttying, either on the wheel or the brush, the latter of which is much the worst, I wear a wet sponge over my mouth and nose, which I have heard from other glass men was a good thing...the putty will get even a little through the sponge...I live at a very healthy place out of the town and think the long walk each way and fresh air must do me

---

[3] *Birmingham Daily Post*, 27 January, 28 January 1859, 27 August 1860, 21 July, 4 December 1862; T. Matsumura, *The Labour Aristocracy Revisited: The Victorian Flint Glassworkers 1850-1880*, (1983), pp. 130-148, for the great strike of 1858-1859.
[4] *BDP*, 23 January 1861, 24 December 1862, 24 March 1863, 13 August 1864.

good. After work I always wash with soap and water and sometimes a little soda. Washing is the grand thing. [5]

The Stones and Fawdry proved themselves to be successful businessmen who could make money. When Fawdry died in June 1867, he was able to leave £2,000 in his will to be distributed amongst local institutions caring for the sick and disabled.[6] Stone, however, wanted to be known as more than just an able businessman. He also wished to be recognised as an expert in glassware, and contributed articles to specialist magazines as well as serving as a juror at an international glass exhibition in London in 1870 and subsequently as such events in Paris in 1878 and Edinburgh in 1886. In recognition of his knowledge of the trade he was elected, in 1882, as the Master of the Worshipful Company of Glass Sellers.

But Stone had his finger in more than one pie. In 1862, with Thomas Bird Smith and Frederick Knight, he bought a paper mill in Duddeston. The repeal of the duties on paper manufacture two years earlier prompted the three men to act, but it was still a risky venture since only Smith, whose uncle was a paper manufacturer, had any previous experience of the trade. Still Stone had great confidence in his own abilities. Smith, Stone & Knight specialized in coarser paper which proved to have a sizeable market; the initial

---

[5] *Fourth Report of Children's Employment Commission,* 1865; *Birmingham Journal,* 23 February 1865; *BDP,* 22 September 1865. The commissioners visited all of the glass houses in Birmingham and the wider area, making the recommendations that women and boys under twelve should not be employed in the manufacturing process and that boys under sixteen should not undertake night work. In 1869, Stone, Fawdry, Stone opened a school for boys in their employment.

[6] *BDP,* 2 July 1867; *BDG,* 24 August 1867. Fawdry (1828-1867) lived at the Poplars in Sheldon and was a churchwarden at St. Giles. He had married Catherine Stone in 1853, but within four years had become a widower; he had subsequently become involved in the restoration of the church, including seeking to install a memorial window to his wife. He left assets of £5,000. His charitable bequests consisted of £500 each to the General Hospital and the Queen's Hospital and £250 each to the Blind Asylum and the Deaf and Dumb Institute: these institutions were funded by legacies, donations, subscriptions and interest from investments.

output of six tons a year gradually increased until the demand necessitated the building of a second paper mill in Nechells in 1873. This expansion was overseen by an able manager, Edwin Parr, who died in March 1878.[7] By his early thirties Stone had established a reputation for himself as an astute businessman and had made some money. He had little difficulty in paying the hefty membership fees of the Geological Society and the Society of Arts.

In 1859 Stone, taking advantage of the seven and twenty-eight day excursion tickets offered by the railway companies, discovered the pleasures of travel. Not until late in life was his wanderlust to diminish. That July he left his home town for the first time on one of the excursion trains run by the London and North Western Railway Company to Llandudno, the favourite holiday destination of the manufacturers and politicians of Birmingham.[8] Feeling an improvement in his health, he soon booked himself onto railway excursions to Weston-Super-Mare and the Lake District, a seven day return to the latter costing him £13. A foreign adventure beckoned and, fluent in French, Stone decided to visit Paris in autumn 1860. During a visit to Norway in 1864 he bought, from a studio in Bergen, his first photograph - a portrait of a young woman in traditional dress. The purchase of this memento marked the beginning of what became a life-time enthusiasm. At this stage Stone had no thoughts of becoming a photographer himself. He collected photographs of places he had visited in the same way that he had earlier collected butterflies or interesting rocks. His appetite for photographs, however, became insatiable, and he began to employ professional photographers, amongst them George Restall and Thomas Lewis. Restall made five contributions to *A History of Lichfield Cathedral* (1870), a 120-page book Stone brought out with his usual serious intent and enthusiasm compensating for his lack of

---

[7] *BDP*, 1 April 1878; *Manchester Courier,* 14 August 1894, for a Smith Stone & Knight advertisement for a manager 'at a two-machine paper mill, one used to M.G. caps preferred'.
[8] *BDG,* 21 July 1860, considers the delights that awaited the visitor from Birmingham at Llandudno.

architectural expertise. [9] Lewis, who opened a studio in Paradise Street in 1872, took photographs of local landmarks such as Castle Bromwich Hall, Aston Hall and St. Martin's Church for Stone. Lewis did not come cheap, but Stone had the money and was able to recoup some of what he had laid out by making a selection of these local pictures available to fifty subscribers at cost price. By 1872, 'at very great expense', Stone had assembled 'one of the largest and most valuable collections of photographs in the midland counties'. [10] A man in possession of a growing collection of photographs wanted to show them off, and that's just what Stone did with an exhibition of 200 photographs he had acquired during a tour of Egypt and Syria in 1869 and during a visit to Paris in 1871 after the destruction of the Commune at the Birmingham and Midland Institute in 1872. [11] At heart, Stone was a collector and that essentially was what he was to remain even when he moved on from buying photographs to taking them himself.

[9] The *Builder*, 5 February 1870, described the publication as 'a superior sort of guidebook' and drew attention to Stone's lack of architectural knowledge whilst the *BDG,* 9 January 1871, was rather more complimentary.

[10] Library of Birmingham, Sir J. B. Stone Newspaper Cuttings, Vol. 1, p. 8.

[11] *Warwickshire Herald,* 17 October 1889, states that Stone commissioned a Parisian photographer to take the pictures - which had a 'peculiar vividness' - depicting the aftermath of the Commune.

2 Family Life

Strong friendships with like-minded men and strong family ties played no small part in the quiet self-assurance and sense of contentment that were the prime elements in the character of John Benjamin Stone. He was very much his father's son – a devout Anglican, an active Tory, a public-spirited man, a shrewd businessman. He greatly admired how his father had transformed his own life. When Benjamin Stone died in 1882, sixty-two years after his arrival in Birmingham, he left very respectable assets of £14,440 and was interred in a family vault he had purchased in Witton Cemetery. Long after they were dead, Stone marked the birthdays of both of his parents by organising family gatherings; in 1902 each family member was presented with a medal featuring a depiction of his father to mark the centenary of his birth. [1]

With his elder half-brother brother James Henry Stone, relations were warm and supportive. When Stone was out of the country or embroiled in conflicts with his workmen, it was invariably his half-brother who publicly defended him. J. H. Stone was a partner in Benton & Stone, a brass house in St. Paul's Square, which manufactured items for the garden including hose pipes, hand pumps and troughs. In 1861, the firm employed forty seven men, twenty one boys and four women. The father of seven children, three of whom pre-deceased him, J. H. Stone lived at Cavendish House in Handsworth. He, too, was a public man – so much so that, when he was thrown from his carriage in November 1885, it made the local Tory daily. One newspaper correspondent offered this mocking appraisal of him:

> Mr Stone is a man of some note in the Conservative Party. He is a borough magistrate (though only appointed by the backstairs influence which prevailed during the evil days of Tory misrule) and his friends claim that he is a man of culture, taste, education and commercial capacity as would fit him to worthily represent his fellows in the town council. More

---

[1] *BDG,* 8 April 1865, for Benjamin Stone's appointment by magistrates as an overseer of the poor in Aston. I am grateful to Roger Stone for letting me inspect the commemorative medal that has been passed down to him.

than all, he is for the moment, and by accident, chairman of the Aston School Board and poses there as the champion of the "religious question".

Chiefly concerned with urging the teaching of the Bible in board schools, J. H. Stone came forward as a Conservative candidate in St. Bartholomew's ward in November 1873 but was roundly defeated. Like his half-brother, he took his public duties seriously, attending, for example, all thirty five meetings of the Aston School Board in 1881.[2]

In June 1867, Stone married Jane Parker, the nineteen year old daughter of a prosperous farmer from Lothersdale in North Yorkshire. Stone had known her for over five years, having met her when arranging for her father Peter Parker to supply lime for his paper mill. In fact it was a double wedding that took place that summer in the small church at Lothersdale: on the same day Thomas Bird Smith married Parker's eldest daughter Ann. It was not uncommon for Victorian manufacturers to strengthen their business arrangements by marriage – the following year Stone's sister Clara married his other partner in the paper mill Frederick Knight. That Peter Parker was also an active supporter of the Conservative cause helped to underpin the new alliance.[3]

Stone now set up home with his new wife–whom he affectionately referred to as Janie - at a house with a large garden they rented in Church Lane in Aston and called Lothersdale. It was here that their six children were born: Ethel (1868); Barron (1869); Dora (1870); Norman (1871); Oscar (1872) and Roland (1876). Jane Stone had uprooted herself and lived well over a hundred miles from her family. In consequence she often made the long journey back to North Yorkshire. With business and political commitments requiring her husband to remain in Birmingham, she grew accustomed to making these journeys with other family members. On returning home by train, in May 1873 accompanied by her niece, she was preventing from continuing the final part of her five-hour journey at Derby by a police officer on suspicion of

---

[2] *BDP*, 26 September, 17 October, 31 October 1873, 19 July 1881, 1 November 1882; *BDG,* 2 November 1885.
[3] *BDG,* 8 June 1867; *BJ,* 8 June 1867; *Leeds Mercury,* 18 January 1896, for Stone waxing lyrical about Yorkshire at a dinner in Birmingham for gentlemen who hailed from that county.

being a fifteen year old girl who had eloped. Embarrassment at the situation fuelled Stone's anger. He vented his spleen in a long letter to *The Times*:

It would appear that the eager anxiety of the police to make so interesting a capture led them to arrest my wife under a supposed resemblance she had to the particulars of the runaway culprit ... A crowd immediately congregated on the platform to curiously survey my wife as if she was some important criminal ... No warrant was produced, no explanation offered and not a particle of consideration was shown by police, guards or porters ... I ... can only view the affair as a gross outrage.

Stone threatened legal action; but, with Edwin Davis, the detective inspector concerned, thoroughly humiliated as his superiors sided with Stone, he accepted an apology and his costs. [4]

Jane Stone was described by one family friend as possessing 'a charming disposition, great amiability and pleasant mannerisms'. [5] She did not share her husband's curiosity about the world. His collections of photographs, rocks, dried flowers and curios held little interest for her, and she did not join him on his travels. When at home, Stone would spend many days on his own in his library absorbed in carefully labelling his collections. Jane, meanwhile, entertained the wives of local gentlemen, including her sister Ann, a near-neighbour at Copeley Park, or visited them in the carriage.

With six children and his ever-growing collections to accommodate, Stone decided to purchase a large house. In November 1877, the family moved to The Grange in Grange Road, Erdington. The area was 'exceptionally quiet, there being few houses and no lamps' – ideal indeed for an 'apparition', which duly appeared at Christmas 1902. [6] Stone's new residence, built on the site of a seventeenth farmhouse by a wealthy Birmingham jeweller, was approached by 'a long carriage drive from Grange Road' and had 'an imposing appearance with a stone and rough cast elevation'.

---

[4] *The Times*, 12 May 1873; Library of Birmingham, Sir J.B. Stone Newspaper Cuttings, I, pp 50-62, for all the correspondence on this matter.

[5] *Sutton Coldfield News*, 1 August 1914

[6] *Worcester Chronicle,* 13 December 1902. The 'apparition' frightened a number of passers-by, but was attributed to a practical joker by the police.

It contained over twenty rooms, including five large bedrooms and the billiard and smoking rooms, library, observatory and fernery were all a Victorian gentleman-scholar might require. Later Stone erected two huts in the grounds to store his photographic plates.[7]

For Stone 'the exceptionally well-fitted library' was the heart of his home. His collection was mostly the standard reference works in his areas of interest, but he did acquire some unusual items. He brought home from Paris in 1871 a run of news-sheets produced during the siege and a number of publications issued by the Communards. 'It is questionable if another set of these journals now exists in the country', the catalogue for the sale of Stone's library in July 1919 noted. He purchased over five hundred copies of the 'extremely rare' seventeenth century periodical the *London Gazette*. He paid £18 for the twenty-one volumes of L. and H. G. Reichenbach's *Icones Florae Germanicae et Helveticae* (1852). Bound in purple morocco with gilt leaves was the 'beautifully written' manuscript of an article called 'The Real Woman in White' by the *Daily Telegraph* journalist George Augustus Sala. In the billiard room Stone hung signed photographs of parliamentarians he had taken, and throughout the house there were landscape watercolours by his friends S. H. Baker and Robert Mann. When The Grange was eventually emptied all sorts of collector's items were put up for sale – a carved rosewood sarcophagus from Egypt, boomerangs from India, carved dishes from Brazil, bamboo umbrellas from China, Zulu shields, the skull of a crocodile.[8]

Life at The Grange, with its spacious grounds (eventually amounting to five-and-half-acres after Stone purchased adjoining land in 1882, 1893 and 1909) and servants, was good. There was a full size tennis court, but Stone's children did spend time away from home. His two daughters, Ethel and Dora, were sent in their early teens to Handsworth Ladies College, where, under the supervision of Mrs Kirkpatrick, they were provided with a basic education and, at an extra cost, lessons in mathematics, singing and dancing. His three eldest sons, Barron, Norman and Oscar, were despatched with their cousins, Parker and Seymour Smith, to Cothill near

---

[7] Library of Birmingham, J. H. Leeson & Son, Catalogue for the Sale of The Grange, March 1919.
[8] Library of Birmingham, J. H. Leeson & Son, Catalogues for the Sale of The Grange, its contents and library, March-July 1919.

Abingdon. An ambition was achieved when Barron Stone passed the entrance examination for Marlborough. Stone wrote regularly to his children at school, advising them on their health, correcting their grammar and consoling Barron on his lowly position in his class at Marlborough. 'It is by no means a serious thing to be bottom at the commencement of term', he informed Barron. 'You will find, when you get more used to the work, that your competition, who look so formidable now, will, one by one, fall off and you will look back and wonder how they could have appeared such strong antagonists'. Stone also encouraged his children to take up botany, declaring himself 'particularly pleased' when Barron began a collection of mosses. Barron, as he contemplated his lessons at Marlborough, was doubtless cheered when his father wrote from a holiday in Switzerland in September 1881 that 'everywhere the grapes and flowers thrive so well...the autumn crocus is flowering in millions of blooms'. [9]

Four live-in servants were usually employed at The Grange and there was also a coach man for his two carriages and gardeners who lived in the vicinity. When the children were young there was a governess as well, in 1881 this being twenty five year old Sarah Brierley. The cook and maids were youthful, with ages in 1871 and 1881 of between seventeen and twenty six; by 1911 the Stones preferred older servants, with two of them aged forty four and fifty seven respectively. Unlike some families who feared gossip about them being passed on, the Stones recruited their servants locally. Advertisements in the local press invited applicants to apply by letter, or for those not confident about their writing skills, to present themselves 'any morning' at The Grange, where they would be seen by Jane Stone. Thus, in April 1884 'a thoroughly good plain cook' was sought; in June 1886 a housemaid who 'must be tall'; and, in August 1890, a sewing maid-waitress, who 'must understand dressmaking'. A genial man in public life, Stone did not hide his displeasure when those who worked for him let him down. 'Cross with the men for neglecting to get the grass cut', he noted in his diary on one occasion. 'Some trouble & annoyance', he recorded

---

[9] Stone Family Papers, Stone to Barron, 18 September 1881, 9 October 1883, 9 February 1884.

when he received an unsolicited delivery of peat, 'Called in the police'. [10]

A highly-knowledgeable amateur botanist who delighted in wild flowers, Stone ensured that his gardens were not over cultivated. 'It was always ... [his] desire', one newspaper reported, 'that the garden around the house should present as wild, and therefore as natural, a state as possible. Instead of formal parterres of bedding plants...masses of burdock...present themselves, not unpicturesquely, to the eye.' To encourage birds, a large number of nesting boxes were placed in the many mature trees. In his diaries Stone often recorded how 'delightful' he found his gardens. 'Letters all day', he wrote with mild irritation on one occasion. 'A few minutes in the garden the whole day'. [11]

Each summer the expansive grounds surrounding The Grange were used to hold garden parties. In July 1886, a garden party celebrated the return of Henry Matthews as MP for East Birmingham. After the speeches, there was 'dancing on the tennis court' and then 'Mr Stone's pretty shrubberies and fruit gardens were...thrown open for inspection'. In July 1888, in spite of 'dripping trees and wet grass', local children danced around a maypole. Their exertions over, the children were served tea by Stone himself. In August 1901, a contingent from the Sutton Coldfield Volunteers, who had recently returned from South Africa, were treated to tea in the gardens and then a speech from Stone, who saw it as his duty to mark their courage. Jane Stone invited women to gatherings at The Grange. In February 1887, she presided over a meeting of 'about thirty of the leading ladies of the district' to make arrangements to mark the Queen's Diamond Jubilee; and in March 1889, she, and a committee of ladies commissioned a silk banner, decorated with symbols associated with Bishop Vesey and the Tudors, for Sutton Coldfield. [12]

---

[10] Census returns, 1871, 1881, 1901, 1911; *BDP*, 8 August 1883, 19 April 1884, 24 June 1886, 10 January 1889, 28 August 1890; Library of Birmingham, Parliamentary Diaries of Sir J. B. Stone, 18 December 1906, 19 July 1908.

[11] *Erdington News*, 11 July 1914; Library of Birmingham, Parliamentary Diaries of Sir J. B. Stone, 18 December 1906, 31 May 1908.

[12] *BDP*, 26 July 1886, 24 February 1887, 24 July, 25 July 1888, 26 March 1889; *Lichfield Mercury,* 1 August 1901.

A busy man, Stone always had much to think about. As he walked through the grounds of The Grange, mulling over his public duties and business interests, he often paused to inspect his fruit and vegetables; he was very proud that his apples and potatoes regularly won prizes. Thinking matters through carefully was a characteristic noted by those who knew Stone well. 'He did things with deliberation', one friend recalled, 'That was part of his character, which may have been taken for pomposity, but I am sure it was not. It was his sense of the orderly. Correctness. I liked him very much...' [13]

---

[13] *BDP*, 2 August 1887; Quoted in B. Jay, *Customs and Faces: The Photographs of Sir Benjamin Stone*, (1972), n.p

3 Glass and Paper

Many of the industrialists of Victorian Birmingham became very wealthy men, able to live extremely comfortably and indulge liberally in their private passions. Joseph Chamberlain created magnificent gardens at his Highbury mansion and, in his many greenhouses, cultivated azaleas, chrysanthemums and, most famously, orchids. Richard Tangye collected Cromwellian memorabilia and travelled to Australia, the United States and South Africa. Samuel Timmins built up an exceptional library of antiquarian volumes and early editions of Shakespeare's plays.[1] Stone's interests were travel and photography. His income was derived from his investments in the manufacture of glass and, particularly, of paper. The death of his partner Frederick Fawdry in 1867 proved to be a turning point for the Union Glassworks in Dartmouth Street. Profits began to decline. Profits of £3189 in 1866 and £2722 in 1867 became profits of £1296 in 1868 and £1062 in 1869. Throughout the 1870s annual profits remained half of what they had been a decade earlier until in 1879, with a loss of £686, the business began to lose money year after year.

Stone addressed these difficulties in a number of ways. In June 1872, when the 22-year old Prince Arthur spent a day visiting the factories of Birmingham, he managed to get the glassworks included in the itinerary. The premises were decorated with green foliage, and galleries were erected to enable the families of the workmen to admire the proceedings. In his hour with Stone, Prince Arthur visited the furnaces, the mixing room and then the engraving shop, seeing a glass tankard manufactured; when completely finished, the tankard was dispatched to him. Stone gained further publicity for the glass house when, in August 1872, members of the Burmese royal family took part in a similar tour. Four years later, the Duke and Duchess of Teck arrived to inspect the premises; 'Fat Mary', though a cousin of Queen Victoria, was short of funds and

---

[1] P. Marsh, *Joseph Chamberlain*, (1984), pp. 139-140; *Oxford Dictionary of National Biography* for entries on Tangye (by W. B. Owen rev. H. C. G. Matthew) and Timmins (by S. Roberts).

left with a sizeable haul of glassware.[2] Stone also sought to promote his business by advertising for an 'energetic' travelling salesman and an agent in London, and by sending his engravers out to demonstrate their skills – for example, at a conversazione of the Moseley and Balsall Heath Literary Association in January 1878.[3] There were also wage cuts. Stone blamed his firm's decline on foreign competition, and at first his workmen accepted these reductions. However, when, in August 1882, Stone announced that he required the glass cutters to bring in and train a boy in their trade, they objected; they were not offered an increase in wages and feared that they would end up putting themselves out of their jobs. It was a bitter dispute: twenty one glass cutters were locked out, two of them having been employed for over fifty years. The Birmingham Trades Council declared that Stone's conduct had been 'monstrous and abominably cruel'; but, apart from appealing for financial assistance for the dismissed glass cutters, there was nothing they could do. Stone, meanwhile, had gone on holiday to Norway.[4]

To mark the Queen's Golden Jubilee in June 1887, a dinner was provided for 3000 elderly people in Birmingham. They were treated to cold beef or ham, hot potatoes, plum pudding, and a tart with 'Jubilee' imprinted on it. This repast was accompanied by a bottle of ginger beer or lemonade, and Stone's firm secured the contract to supply 3000 tumblers for the revellers.[5] Stone, however, was unable to turn round its fortunes. The losses that year were £1407, and they continued until, in 1890, he sold the business at a value well below its worth as a going concern to another glass manufacturer, James Stevens & Sons. Stone may well have been connected with the firm for forty years, but, in business, he felt no

---

[2] *BDP*, 25 June, 16 August 1872; *BDG,* 11 August, 2 September 1876. Prince Arthur, (1850-1942) was the third son of Queen Victoria. His main interest was the army.
[3] *BDP*, 14 December 1874, 3 January 1876, 14 January 1880, 25 April, 24 December 1882. For advertisements for 'a respectable woman used to wiping out glass. 8s a week', lapidaries and warehousemen see *BDP*, 24 June 1874, 22 December 1880, 22 October 1886, 6 February 1889, 13 January, 4 February, 28 May, 31 July 1890.
[4] *BDP*, 4 September, 5 September 1882; Library of Birmingham, Sir J. B. Stone Newspaper Cuttings, 2, p. 28.
[5] *BDP*, 18 June 1887.

sentimentality; what he felt in fact was an 'eager desire to get quit of it'.[6]

If the glass house was losing money, the paper mills in Duddeston, Nechells and Aston most certainly were not. Smith, Stone & Knight employed well over one hundred workmen. Advertisements for youths to assist with grinding knives and loading wagons, for men to make paper bags and for clerks regularly appeared in the local newspapers. Wages varied from 4 1/2d an hour for those working with steam boilers to 30s a week for clerical work. [7] The workmen took part in the custom of collecting money for local charitable causes – for example, £1.1s and £2.2s were sent to the Eye Hospital in November 1883 and June 1894.[8] Relations between Stone and his colleagues and their employees were satisfactory until, in April 1886, wage cuts of 33 per cent were announced. The justification for such a severe reduction in wages was the falling price of paper. The workmen argued that the costs for materials used by the firm had also fallen. None of the other paper mills in Birmingham were cutting wages, and it was undoubtedly a provocative step. Nonetheless Stone's employees offered to consider a smaller reduction. The workmen in all three mills began a strike, declaring at a meeting at the New Inn Assembly Rooms in Nechells that, after Stone and his colleagues had refused to meet them, that there would be no further concessions. Stone got his way, and his employees got a cricket team and an annual trip to Blackpool: in July 1893 they left Birmingham at 5.00am on the Saturday and returned at 2.30 am on the Sunday. [9]

There were deaths and injuries in the paper mills: a nineteen year old boy suffered a terrible fate after being pulled into machinery in August 1886; a fourteen year old boy died after being struck on the head when a grindstone splintered in February 1890 (his father was awarded £20 compensation for negligence); a worker killed in April 1893 left a widow and ten children (a fund was started for them); and a fifteen year old girl had a foot amputated

---

[6] Scrapbook in the possession of the Stone family, p. 248.
[7] *BDP*, 31 January, 1 May, 21 September 1874, 2 February 1882, 19 November 1883.
[8] *BDP*, 29 January, 16 May 1881, 16 November 1883, 18 May 1893, 27 June 1894, 4 January 1900.
[9] *BDP*, 2 April 1886, 28 May 1894; *BDG,* 22 July 1893.

after an accident in September 1893. When Henry Stephens, a carpenter, lost the sight of one eye in 1900, he was awarded, under the recently-passed Workmen's Compensation Act, £1 a week; when he declined to return to permanent work on the grounds that his injury caused giddiness and headaches, the sum was reduced to 8s a week.[10]

In March 1894, Smith, Stone & Knight became a registered company with capital of £150,000 in 10s shares. Stone's sons Barron and Oscar and Smith's sons Parker and Seymour now became fully involved. The business was certainly making money, with Smith able to contribute £1000 to the building of a mission hall at St. Clement's in Nechells; but personal relations between the owners were deteriorating.[11] Stone and Smith were soon embroiled in an increasingly bitter dispute over the ownership of a patent to a new paper pulverizer. Stone brought in his solicitors, warning them that, 'I am being trifled with and I can assure you I am in no trifling humour'. The disagreements were not resolved until 1902 when Stone, weary of it all, sold his interest in the pulverizer patent. The damage in relations between the two families was not to be repaired. Following Smith's death in 1905, a new dispute broke out between his son and successor Parker Smith and Stone. A series of 'strained negotiations' followed, with Parker Smith being, in Stone's words, 'rude and unfair'. Stone had had enough. In October 1906 the paper mills passed firmly into the control of Parker and Seymour Smith, who became chairman and a director respectively after Stone resigned as a director and sold them the majority of his shares for £13,000. Though Stone no longer had a say in the business, he did manage to secure for Barron a seat on the board and for Oscar the post of manager, and place the remaining £6000 of his shares in trust for reversion to his sons on his death. In 1927,

---

[10] *BDP*, 13 August 1886, 1 February, 11 July 1890, 12 April, 14 September 1893, 1 August 1900; *BDP*, 15 March 1884, 21 July 1888, for fines of 10s for emitting black smoke from the chimneys of the Nechells mill.
[11] *Worcester Journal,* 29 February 1896.

after another acrimonious dispute, Barron was forced out of the company.[12]

The glass works and paper mills were not Stone's only business investments. In 1875 he provided capital for the Spon Lane Colliery Company in the Black Country, serving as vice-chairman on a board of five. In the first year buildings, roads, a tramway and a wharf were constructed, and the directors looked forward to the mining of coal that was 'as bright as pitch...as good as any collier could wish to stick his pike in.' When the anticipated thick coal seam had not been reached after two years, the shareholders became disgruntled. A concerned Stone informed them that each director 'felt that his honour and judgement were at stake' and that they 'would not give way without a sacrifice of their reputation'. One year later, with the coal seam still not being exploited, he offered the reassurance that he himself remained 'exceedingly cheerful'. 'The present moment was not a good time to start in the coal trade', he informed the shareholders, 'but something would "turn up" and give them a chance of trading success'. And something did turn up: in March 1878 the directors were relieved to inform shareholders that the coal seam had been reached. The seam, however, was not as thick as had been anticipated and the business had run out of money. A committee of shareholders conducted an investigation, blaming both the colliery manager and the board: the manager had issued misleading reports and had 'sought to raise a cloud of dust to obstruct or avoid their more direct and pertinent enquiries' whilst the board had knowingly been taken in. After four years the Spon Lane Colliery Company entered voluntary liquidation. Stone had not only lost a great deal of money but had suffered the humiliation in business he had been anxious to avoid.[13]

This disappointment did not prevent Stone from looking for new investments. In 1881, he bought shares in, and became a

---

[12] *BDP*, 14 March 1894; Library of Birmingham, Pulverizer Papers, p. 48; Library of Birmingham, Parliamentary Diaries of Sir J. B. Stone, 8 October, 17 October 1906. Though taken over more than once, the firm continues to operate

[13] *BDP*, 6 March, 20 March 1875, 8 February 1876, 3 February, 6 February, 1 September 1877, 26 February 1878, 27 March, 1 April 1879. *BDP*, 20 January 1881, 3 May 1884.

director of, the Employers' Liability and Workpeople's Accident and Provident Insurance Company, set up following legislation to safeguard working people from industrial injury. This time he enjoyed a measure of success: premium income increased from £3,524 in 1881-1882 to £6,833 in 1883-1884 and the company was able to pay out a dividend of 10 per cent. [14] In 1883 Stone, with two other investors, bought for £18,500 the long-established Old Union Mill Flour and Bread Company, which, because of antiquated machinery, had been unable to pay dividends to its 500 shareholders, of which Stone was one. The firm was successfully re-launched, but Stone's involvement did not last long. [15]

With his relations with T. B. Smith very fraught by the mid-1890s, Stone's desire to invest in other enterprises grew stronger. He became involved at this time in the construction of a railway in South Africa, in the quarrying of granite in Leicestershire and in the building of shopping arcades and houses in Birmingham. Stone had seen for himself the considerable scope for development in South Africa during a visit in 1894. In May 1896, he became president of the Natal-Zululand Railway Company which was formed with a capital of £350,000 to finance the building of a fifty mile railway from Verulam to the river Tugela. This was excellent farming country and, at first, it seemed a promising investment: in December 1897 the first ten miles of the railway were opened. Thereafter the project ran into difficulties, particularly with recruiting labourers; the remaining section of the railway had still not been completed when Stone resigned from the board in 1900.[16]

More profitable for Stone were his investments in the Cliffe Hill Granite Company in Leicestershire and in the City Arcades Company that was formed to build a series of shopping arcades in the centre of Birmingham. Established in November 1894 with Stone one of its four directors, Cliffe Hill was from the outset a commercially successful enterprise. 'Good year's trading', Stone noted with satisfaction in his diary after attending the annual meeting in August 1906. Glass-roofed and with ornate entrances and an underground passage for the delivery of goods to the 100

---

[14] *BDP*, 20 January 1881, 3 May 1884.

[15] *BDP*, 29 June, 18 November 1882, 22 May, 16 October, 20 October, 6 November 1883, 21 August 1884, 9 October 1891.

[16] *Hull Daily Mail,* 3 July 1896; *Morning Post,* 2 November 1897.

shops, City Arcades was a major undertaking. Stone was chairman of the company, and amongst the other four directors were his fellow MP Birmingham Ebenezer Parkes and H. L. Tangye, son of Richard Tangye. By February 1900 shop rents were generating £5,000 a year with the expectation that, when the work was complete, revenue would exceed £17-18,000. [17] Meanwhile, on the south side of Bunbury Road in Northfield, roads, including two named after his sons Barron and Norman, were constructed after Stone bought the land, deemed 'absolutely ripe for building', at an auction at the Grand Hotel in April 1894. He then constructed houses, which by 1901 were occupied by professional families, employing one or two servants.[18]

When Stone died in July 1914 he left assets – that is his total wealth including property – of £68,051. He had, after 1906, withdrawn from his main business interest of paper manufacturing, but still earned money from other investments, including in property and quarrying. He was comfortably off, but not as wealthy as some of the other Birmingham industrialists – Chamberlain and Tangye left assets of, respectively, £126,019 and £226,319. Inevitably, Stone had encountered setbacks during his long career in business, including the selling off of the glass house after it piled up losses and his disastrous investment in the coal mine. His reputation for business prowess and financial expertise, however, was the major reason why he was so often put forward for public office. Though Stone's name was regularly seen on the subscription lists to such institutions as the Children's Hospital or the Bluecoat School, he was never a major contributor to philanthropic causes. It is impossible to calculate how much Stone invested in his interests, but it was undoubtedly a substantial sum. For twenty years he employed professional photographers, and, when he took up photography himself, he recruited men to assist him and seemingly placed no limits on the number of pictures he took. On top of this there were the expensive expeditions abroad. Stone made money - but he also spent it.

---

[17] *BDP*, 12 January, 12 February, 17 August 1900. *Birmingham Evening Mail*, 25 March 1972, for the restoration of one of these arcades; Library of Birmingham, Parliamentary Diaries of Sir J. B. Stone, 22 August 1906.
[18] *BDP*, 27 January, 29 March, 7 July 1894.

4 A Conservative

In a phrase that was subsequently widely-quoted, John Bright, who represented Birmingham in Parliament for thirty-two years, observed that 'if you go to the sea nearly anywhere you like, and take up a spoonful of water, it will be salt; if you return a Member for any district of Birmingham, he will be Liberal'. [1] Birmingham was indeed a proudly Liberal town. With one exception, when personal rivalries in the radical camp let in the Tory Richard Spooner in 1844, the two MPs returned to represent the town were Liberals. When John Bright was nominated as an MP in 1857, it was to strengthen the town's reputation as a Liberal stronghold of national importance. Stone certainly did not join in the celebrations when Bright arrived in Birmingham. Stone was a Conservative, or a Liberal-Conservative, as the local Conservative and Whig opponents of Bright styled themselves in the 1860s.

Stone had learned his political opinions from his father. He believed in defending the constitution and the established church. Both father and son were prominent members of the congregation of St. Matthew's Church, erected in Duddeston by the Birmingham Church Building Society in 1840. Stone regularly visited the adjoining school room, and, in 1865, was a moving force in founding a mutual improvement society associated with the church, awarding in that first year a volume of Tennyson's verse to the working man whose essay most impressed him. [2] Throughout his life Stone believed that the Conservatives were the natural friends of working people. Stone was not a political orator, leaving speech-making to others if he possibly could. He believed strongly that the Conservative cause was often handicapped by poor organisation, and his political work was to be principally in this area. From the

---

[1] *BDP*, 31 October 1868.
[2] *BDP*, 9 February 1866; *BDG*, 22 April 1865, 28 December 1867, for Christmas celebrations at St. Matthew's at which Stone 'gratified a large company with the effects produced by a new philosophical toy'. Also *BDP*, 14 April 1870, 13 February 1873 for Stone's lectures to, respectively, the Bloomsbury and Nechells Christian Association and the Church of England Young Men's Association.

mid-1870s Stone became the leading figure in challenging the Liberal ascendancy in Birmingham.

To promote his notion of Conservatism Stone helped found, in 1866, the Birmingham Working Men's Liberal-Conservative Association. He and his father were vice-presidents of the Duddeston-cum-Nechells branch. In August 1867 Stone chaired a lecture in the ward by H. C. Edwards entitled 'Our Constitutional Inheritance', prefacing the main event with the observation that 'they banded themselves together against the tyranny of democracy– one of the greatest of tyrannies'. [3] In November 1868, when the banker Sampson Lloyd and the newspaper editor Sebastian Evans contested Birmingham in the Conservative cause, Stone chaired the election committee in Duddeston-cum-Nechells, and contributed £5 to the campaign fund. When Lloyd and Evans were swept aside by the ruthless Birmingham Liberal Association, Stone could only look on in admiration; there was a lesson to be learned in his ward, he reflected, where they had more promises than the Liberals but had not been able to get their vote out.[4]

Though well-known as a Conservative, it was as a respected local businessman and resident that Stone's name was put forward for election to the town council in May 1869. 'Vote for Stone! Vote for Stone! Who is sure to go to the poll', his newspaper advertisements proclaimed. George Page, an iron-founder, appeared as a Liberal, though one of the Liberal councillors George Wilkinson declared for Stone. Stone's committee brushed aside the challenge as 'a farce' and made speeches that were 'strongly depreciatory of Mr Page'. Stone secured a handsome victory, securing 652 votes to Page's 183. Page used the declaration of the result to get his own back on those who had taunted him, declaring that a better candidate than himself did not exist. Stone was elected without any effort of his own. He was in fact in Egypt. It was his brother J. H. Stone who thanked the electors, and the Liberals were soon complaining that he had not formally accepted office. Stone heard the result three weeks later, declaring his pleasure at 'this unsolicited honour'. [5] In truth Stone, whilst happy to take a leading

---

[3] *BDG*, 17 August 1867; *BDP*, 20 August 1867; *Birmingham Journal,* 18 January 1868.
[4] *BDP*, 3 November 1868.
[5] *BDP*, 16 May, 20 May, 21 May, 22 May, 16 June, 17 June 1869.

role as an organiser and to chair meetings, never demonstrated much eagerness to put himself forward as a candidate, and it cannot be said that he leapt into action in the most critical contested election he was involved in–the stiff fight to hold onto his parliamentary seat in East Birmingham in 1906.

Doubtless to his relief Stone did not face any further contests before his retirement as a town councillor in 1878. The role of councillor suited him – he liked committee work and he had a sincere desire to play a part in the governance of his home town. One committee he served on looked after the small Art Gallery which had opened in August 1867. Stone spoke out against the opening of the Art Gallery on Sundays and the purchase of a collection of Chinese and Japanese artefacts on the grounds that 'the property would not prove of the slightest benefit to the working classes of the town'. He clearly did not feel the same about a donation of his own, a carefully-crafted glass vase, 'the single most beautiful piece of glass in existence', in his words. Stone's desire to improve his town was made clear in his efforts to get the London and North Western Railway Company to upgrade the railway station at Aston in September 1876. The situation, he informed the chairman Richard Moon, was dangerous – there was 'horrifying' overcrowding and, after buying a ticket, some passengers had to cross the railway lines. Moon complained that 'no one ever thought of coming forward with any money', but grudgingly agreed to build new accommodation for passengers at a cost of £2,700. [6]

When elected, Stone was the only Conservative on the council and, in spite of his best efforts to promote organisation, he had, five years later, been joined by just six more. With forty one councillors in 1874, the Liberals were the masters of Birmingham. Though a shareholder in the Birmingham Waterworks Company, Stone did not in fact object in principle to the municipalization of the gas and water supplies. He knew full well that it was against the spirit of the age to contest the argument of Joseph Chamberlain that public services should be owned by the public. What Stone did do, however, was to raise questions over the cost. Speaking of the municipal purchase of the gas supply, there was, he declared in April 1874, 'not half an hour's discussion of the merits of the terms themselves'. He illustrated his arguments about prudence in

---

[6] *BDP*, 6 October 1869, 5 August 1874; *BDG*, 30 September 1876.

expenditure with stories such as one about a sewage farm where 'after spending a large sum of money upon a plough, it was put on a soft quagmire where it has disappeared and nothing more has been heard of it.' By March 1877, Stone was warning that the debt of the council was increasing at a rate of £120,000 each year. [7]

Outside the council chamber Stone was sharper in his condemnation of the Liberals. 'The radicals of Birmingham had always assumed an amount of importance that did not belong to them, he declared in January 1878. 'They formed a small but noisy section; they were demonstrative and very presuming of their own importance'. Stone encouraged the establishment of Conservative Working Men's Clubs and attended meetings of an organisation called the Duddeston Labour Representation League - though this did not exist to actually elect a working class councillor for Stone himself 'claimed to be the representative of the working man'. He confidently declared that 'speaking from personal intimate acquaintance with the working men of this district, I may say that the time has gone by when they are to be led or frightened into believing that Liberal leaders are their only safe and trusty friends'. [8]

For all Stone's optimism, the political landscape of Birmingham remained unchanged. The Tory Eight, who campaigned for religious instruction in the School Board elections in November 1873, managed to recruit the boys of King Edward's as canvassers but still went down to defeat. In the parliamentary election of 1874 Stone had no desire to be the Conservative candidate and could not persuade any one else to come forward. Five years later, in the November elections, only three Conservative candidates appeared in the sixteen wards, and discovered that even free pints of beer handed out by local brewers could not stave off defeat. [9] In truth, the ward committees of the BCA mostly existed on paper only – Stone might urge their creation, the paid organiser William Barton might set them up, but they soon folded. All of this greatly amused the local Liberal newspapers and satirical magazines. When Stone organised one meeting at the town hall, the *Birmingham Daily Post* mocked the empty seats and early departures whilst the *Dart* published a cartoon of him addressing a

[7] *BDP*, 22 September 1870, 1 April 1874, 1 March 1877.
[8] *BDP*, 5 March 1873, 24 January 1878, 27 July 1875.
[9] *BDP*, 11 June, 7 November, 17 November 1873.

ward meeting in Duddeston with only 'Mrs Aris'– the Conservative - supporting *Birmingham Daily Gazette* – present. Stone was in fact a favourite target of the *Dart*. 'How would he...like it if his only matrimonial hope was his grandmother?', it observed after Stone had, at a public meeting in Duddeston in March 1877, urged young women to choose only Tories for their sweethearts.[10]

But Stone did not retreat to his glassworks and photographs. In Disraeli he saw the perfect Conservative leader. Here was a man who, with his emphasis on the responsibilities of the wealthy towards the poor, offered the Conservatives an identity and electoral appeal. Very early on, perhaps before many other Conservatives, Stone saw what Disraeli offered their cause. To his great delight he managed to get two of Disraeli's ministers – the Home Secretary Richard Cross in November 1876 and the Chancellor of the Exchequer Sir Stafford Northcote in October 1878 - to address meetings in the Liberals' own backyard. Stone lavished praise in his warm-up speeches on Cross' Artisans Dwellings Act, which was being put into use in Birmingham to clear slums, and declared that, though elections were 'not always pleasant', they could return a Conservative MP. Cross echoed the sentiment; Northcote was undoubtedly amused to be defending a Conservative government 'in the heart of enemy country'. [11]

When, in summer and autumn 1876, Disraeli's policy in the Balkans came under ferocious criticism from Gladstone and the Liberals, Stone came out fighting. The moralistic stance Disraeli's critics were taking irked him. Of course, the massacres by Turkish irregular forces in Bulgaria should be condemned, but the anti-Turkish agitation convulsing the country was 'unpatriotic' and 'dangerous' and 'not only harassed the government but...had the dangerous probability of leading them into a European war'.[12] Though he got on well enough with leading local Liberals – even if from time to time antagonisms did flare up – Stone loathed what he

---

[10] *BDP,* 1 March 1877; The *Dart,* 24 March 1877. The *Lantern* was a short-lived satirical magazine that supported the Tories, but no copies appear to have survived.
[11] *BDP*, 21 November, 22 November 1876; *The Times*, 21 October 1878; Library of Birmingham, J. B. Stone Newspaper Cuttings, XVI, for tickets, leaflets and correspondence relating to Northcote's visit
[12] *BDP*, 5 October 1876.

believed Liberalism stood for. Liberalism, he decided, deserved nothing less than to be confronted in its stronghold. In the parliamentary election of 1880 he attempted to do just that.

Stone resisted overtures that he came forward; but he did not need to look far for a standard bearer. The Tory Chief Whip knew of a man itching to taunt Chamberlain in his own town. Fred Burnaby (1842-1885) was a soldier-adventurer, reputedly the strongest man in the British army and the author of two best-selling books describing his exploits on horseback in Russia and Asia Minor.[13] For Stone he was just the man: admired, flamboyant and an ardent defender of Disraeli's foreign policy. For Burnaby, Birmingham was the place to make his political name. Burnaby was Stone's guest at The Grange in May 1878, and two months later was formally adopted as a Conservative candidate for Birmingham. Stone publicly speculated that a working man might join him on the Tory ticket, but in the end it was an uninspiring local toff, the Hon. Augustus Calthorpe.

The Liberal-supporting local satirical weeklies could barely believe their luck when Burnaby was adopted, one of them greeting the announcement with a series of fictional letters describing how Stone got his man:

Dear Captain Burnaby,

We must have a Conservative candidate. You are fixed upon as the person to receive that honour. We must have a stranger as no one who knows anything of the locality and who remembers previous contested elections is inclined to fight ... Lowe will help you get up your election speeches.

Yours etc

J. B. Stone

---

[13] Burnaby's books were *A Ride to Khiva*, (1876) and *On Horseback Through Asia Minor*, (1877). See S. Roberts 'A Ride to Birmingham: Fred Burnaby's Election Campaign of 1880' in *BMI Insight: The Journal of the Birmingham and Midland Institute and Library*, no. 9, (2011), pp. 34-37.

Dear Mr Stone,

Don't mind going in for an election lark. Nothing on hand just now...You can announce me as soon as you like'

Yours etc

F. Burnaby

Dear Captain Burnaby,

Great enthusiasm on receipt of your letter. You are the most popular man in Birmingham. Wadham is going to buy a copy of your book and Nock, who says he has read it, thinks it the finest work in the English language, next to a little work of mine entitled *A Tour Through Spain* and of which I shall be proud to present you with a copy when you are a member for Birmingham.

Yours etc

J. B. Stone [14]

Burnaby became a regular guest at Stone's home, where he wrote and rehearsed his public speeches. He made his debut on a political platform in Birmingham in April 1879, and a few months later attended a garden party at The Grange. The heavy rain that led to the abandonment of the garden party dampened Stone but not his spirits. He continually talked up Burnaby's prospects. 'With the efforts of thousands and thousands of supporters in the town', he declared, 'he was quite sure victory was in their reach...' During the campaign in March 1880, Burnaby did everything Stone wanted of him. He called for trade tariffs. He condemned high rates. But mostly he argued that patriotism and honour demanded support for Disraeli's policy towards Russia. Burnaby and Calthorpe were defeated, trailing Chamberlain, the third-placed Liberal, by almost 4,000 votes. Based on canvass returns, Stone had genuinely

---

[14] The *Town Crier,* August 1878. Interestingly, Stone had discussed with Sydney Gedge (1802-1883), second master at King Edward's during his time there and admired in the town for his work with the Church Missionary Society, the possibility of coming forward in the Conservative cause.

expected an upset, believing that Burnaby would secure first or second place and Calthorpe third place. A few months later he resigned as president of the BCA, and was succeeded by the tinplate manufacturer J. Satchell Hopkins. In ensuing elections the Liberal press was never slow to remind Stone of the bullish comments he had made that year.[15]

For Stone the Conservative challenge in 1880 had been about 'the political freedom of the town' as much as about a vindication of Disraeli's foreign policy. 'The Conservative Party formed a powerful minority in Birmingham', he declared 'and had a right to expect some representation'. [16] Everywhere he looked Stone saw the firm hand of the BLA. He made an attempt to prevent the council of the Birmingham and Midland Institute remaining an adjunct of the BLA by nominating four Conservatives, including Satchell Hopkins; but his men failed to be elected. To confront the Liberals Stone continued to call for better party organisation, lending support to the newly-established Conservative Associations in Sutton Coldfield (1883) and Erdington (1884). He also joined the council of the National Union of Conservative Associations, which held a conference in Birmingham in September 1883. [17]

Stone's involvement in the Conservative Party was beginning to extend beyond Birmingham. He was consulted by Lord Randolph Churchill about the launch, in November 1883, of the Primrose League which aimed to attach working class voters, particularly in urban areas like Birmingham, to the imperialist and Conservative causes. Churchill initially favoured a secret society with principles but no plan of action, but, Stone informed him, this would be 'a worthless effort'; instead he argued that the creation of 'a Tory Patriotic League...with a very carefully prepared scheme...[could] be made of enormous use to the Conservative Party'. Several habitations, as local branches were known, were established in Birmingham, including a Burnaby Habitation and a Dames' Habitation, which sought to encourage women to get involved in canvassing. It was the sort of populist political operation that Stone

---

[15] *BDP*, 31 March 1880. Also see *BDP*, 12 March, 29 March, 13 July 1880.
[16] *BDP*, 31 March 1880, October 1883.
[17] *BDP*, 23 November 1882, 10 February, 2 October, 13 November 1883, 5 March 1884.

believed in; but recruitment was slow with no more than twenty attending a dinner in April 1885 to mark Disraeli's birthday (Primrose Day). [18]

Stone's wider role was also evident in his participation in the Midland Conservative Union. This body organised a demonstration, with Churchill, Northcote and Burnaby accepting invitations to speak, in support of the House of Lords in Aston Park in October 1884. The House of Lords had obstructed the Liberal bill to extend the franchise, demanding that a redistribution of parliamentary seats also take place. Roused by Chamberlain's call for 'a serious collision' between the Lords and the Commons, Stone's language was strong: the 'virulent' and 'insidious' comments of Chamberlain represented an intention 'to exterminate' the House of Lords; 'they, as a Conservative Party, did not mean to have the constitution tampered in that way', he declared. [19] Such was the determination of Stone and the Conservatives to rally opposition to Chamberlain in his own town that they took the risk of organising an open-air meeting, though admission was still by ticket. On the day a Liberal counter-demonstration took place only a few hundred yards away, and the rival factions clashed; only two people were seriously injured but, as the Conservative fireworks were set off, chairs, platforms and walls were destroyed. Accused by Chamberlain of inciting the rioting, Stone angrily informed the Liberal *Daily News* that 'if he means to imply that I either hired roughs, knew of roughs being hired or that I in any way countenanced such a disreputable proceeding, I have to give the statement my most unqualified and indignant denial'.[20]

In the North Warwickshire by-election in July 1884, the Conservative candidate Albert Muntz - younger son of the Birmingham Liberal MP George Muntz - topped the poll. Stone

---

[18] Library of Birmingham, 150 Stray Letters, Vol. 1, Stone to Churchill, 26 November, 11 December 1883; *BDP*, 5 July, 27 November 1884, 20 April, 26 October, 31 October 1885, 13 April 1886. The Burnaby Habitation reported that it had 131 members in April 1886, 57 of them 'knights'.

[19] *BDP*, 29 August 1884, *The Times*, 15 October 1884.

[20] *Daily News*, 1 November 1884; John A. Bridges *Reminiscences of a Country Politician*, (1906), pp. 136-147, for a detailed, first-hand account of the 'Aston Riots'.

had joined in canvassing in the final days of the campaign, and was delighted. Nonetheless he remained unsure about Lord Randolph Churchill's intention to put himself forward as a candidate to take on John Bright in the newly-created Central Birmingham constituency. He feared defeat would damage Churchill's prospects of political advancement. But Churchill fought with determination and energy. He made regular visits to the constituency, and in his speeches pledged support for land and local government reform and a vigorous foreign policy. 'I like your husband', one voter told Churchill's wife, 'and I like what he says. But I can't throw John Bright off like an old coat'. Bright held on in November 1885, but only by 773 votes. Forgetting his original doubts, Stone declared that the Conservatives had achieved 'a virtual victory'. A relieved Liberal press seized on his words:

> Quoth Rowlands: This looks very blue;
> Poor Churchill – what a sell,
> I think I'll have a brandy hot,
> And forthwith pulled the bell;
> While Stone sat still with stony stare,
> Gazing profoundly on the air.

> But soon he gave a sudden jerk,
> And pulled his pencil out,
> And figured over several sheets,
> Then raised a joyous shout;
> Ah, ah, 'tis not so bad you see,
> We've won a virtual victory.

> 'Tis true that Bright is just ahead,
> By hundreds nine to ten,
> But I can show he should have won,
> By just as much again;
> We've lowered their proud majority
> And that's a virtual victory.[21]

---

[21] *BDP*, 27 June, 3 July 1884; Library of Birmingham, Sir J. B. Stone Newspaper Cuttings, Vol. 2, p. 52; Robert Rhodes James, *Lord Randolph Churchill*, (1986 edn.), pp. 213-214; R. F. Foster, *Lord Randolph Churchill*, (1988), pp. 236-239

It seemed to Stone that the level of support for the Conservatives in Birmingham entitled them to a say in the governance of the town. To secure this he was not averse to doing deals with the Liberals. Thus, in March 1879, he avoided contests for the sixty places on the Birmingham Board of Guardians by agreeing to the Liberals nominating forty one and the Conservatives nineteen members respectively.[22] Stone himself devoted several days a month to public work. From 1882 until 1887, he served as chairman of the Aston Board of Guardians, and from 1884 until 1889 as chairman of its subsidiary the Aston Rural Sanitary Authority, which looked after drainage arrangements. He urged that elections should be avoided in the selection of the twenty eight members of the Board of Guardians. They were, he declared, 'public men doing public business.' When the possibility of a woman joining the Board arose, there was resistance from Stone. 'Personally', he observed, 'he considered the character of the work of such a nature that a lady could not enter into it with the same zest and power that a gentleman could'. Meetings took place fortnightly and were usually harmonious, though the antagonisms Stone hoped to avoid did on occasions arise. In April 1885, the long-serving T. F. Adams objected to Stone's re-election as chairman and pointed out that his name had never been put forward for vice-chairman. [23]

The Aston Board of Guardians was responsible for a very large area – Aston, Curdworth, Minworth, Sutton Coldfield and Wishaw – and supported about 1600 people, at a cost of over £750 a year, with outdoor relief whilst the population in the workhouse in Gravelly Lane was never much short of 800. Stone wanted the whole operation to be run as economically as possible but believed it was his Christian duty 'to have everything done decently and with due regard to the feelings of the poor people with whom they had to deal'. He joined, in January 1885, a town committee soliciting subscriptions to help the growing numbers of unemployed. The funds raised were used to provide unemployed men with work breaking stones and digging in parks and to distribute 2000 pairs of boots and other essential items. By September, £3,797 had been

---

[22] *BDP*, 8 March 1879.
[23] *BDP*, 11 April 1884, 29 April, 16 September 1885.

raised and 8,817 poor people given help, Stone ensuring that the Aston Board of Guardians made use of the fund.[24]

During these years Stone also sat as a magistrate at Aston Police Court. Very few of those who appeared before him and his colleagues were discharged. And so a man who engaged in 'furious driving in Aston Road' was fined 10s, a milk seller who added water to milk was fined 40s, a boy who stole from his employer received six strokes of the birch and a man who stole 400 bricks was sentenced to six months imprisonment with hard labour. Those facing more serious offences were sent to Warwick Assizes. One of these was Thomas Milnes Lockett 'a gentlemanly-looking man' accused of forgery and embezzlement in his role as a ledger clerk in Stone's own paper mills; he was eventually imprisoned for five years. Servants stealing watches, boys not paying rail fares and paupers destroying their workhouse suits all had their punishments meted out to them. However, when a glass manufacturer, was accused of indecently assaulting his servant, the case was thrown out after the young woman 'contradicted herself repeatedly'.[25]

There were, of course, men other than Stone who were involved in promoting the Conservative cause in Birmingham in the 1870s and in the first half of the 1880s. John Lowe, for example, often spoke at Conservative meetings throughout the 1870s, though by 1880 his opponents were reporting that 'he has been kept so in the background lately we thought he had emigrated'. The solicitor Joseph Rowlands also became prominent after 1879, and was responsible for the invitation to Churchill to stand in the town. But it was Stone who during these years was more than any other figure, the local face of Conservatism. It was Stone who, in spite of the setbacks and the defeats, kept the Conservative cause alive, invited the national speakers, insisted that the election that came in 1880

---

[24] *BDP*, 3 May, 28 June 1882, 16 September, 26 September 1885.

[25] *BDP*, 11 January, 18 January, 22 February, 12 April 1877, 10 April, 17 April, 18 December 1878, 9 August 1883, 15 May 1884; *Manchester Evening News,* 23 March 1877. Thomas Milnes Lockett had 'failed in life', falling into debt in Manchester in 1866. He had been taken on, on a salary of 4 guineas a week, by Smith, Stone and Knight in 1872; he was 45 years old at the time he was accused by his employer of forging cheques. For other cases of attempts to defraud Smith, Stone & Knight, see *Staffordshire Sentinel,* 23 August 1877, *BDP,* 15 April 1891.

had to be contested. It was Stone, who so impressed by the BLA, repeatedly urged the Conservatives to create a similar organisation. Stone did all this because he believed deeply that the country's institutions should be protected from Liberal attack. He also did it because he also recognised what others perhaps did not – that in the great Liberal stronghold of Birmingham, there were Conservative voices and they deserved to be heard. [26]

[26] *BDP*, 12 March 1880; *Birmingham Faces and Places*, I (1889), pp. 13-14, for a portrait of Rowlands.

5 The Amateur Photographer

Late Victorian Britain hummed with the energy of the amateur enthusiast – men with money who, largely self-taught, wrote books about botany, butterflies and fossils, newspaper columns about local history, built observatories, conducted archaeological digs and oversaw the restoration of churches. Stone was such a man. He would have enjoyed conversations about any of these matters; but it is with photography that his name will chiefly be associated. Though he admired 'the men who...by little tricks...got over difficulties' and always himself used the latest methods of development, Stone was not particularly interested in the technical aspects of photography–he employed assistants to help him with this - nor did he take pictures of his many friends unless they had achieved some sort of eminence.[1] Stone saw the camera as a way of preserving for posterity centuries-old buildings, documents and customs before they disappeared. His was very much a quest to embalm all the evidence he could find of national identity. He had no doubts that it was work of considerable importance. From time-to-time Stone did overstate his own significance in this enterprise. Stone did not invent the concept of record photography, did not read the first papers to local scientific societies on the subject and clearly was not responsible for surveys undertaken, in 1888-9, by photographic societies in Birkenhead, Sheffield and Manchester. With his eye on posterity, he annotated his earlier photographic albums in a way that perhaps conveyed the impression that he had actually taken the photographs himself. In fact Stone had been collecting photographs for a quarter of a century before he himself took up photography. It seems that Stone did not become an active photographer until the late 1880s.[2]

It was, as Peter James has written in an important essay, William Jerome Harrison (1845-1908) who first urged that the amateur photographers of Birmingham make a survey of their local

---

[1] *BDP*, 9 January 1895.
[2] *Warwickshire Herald,* 17 October 1889; Library of Birmingham, Sir J. B. Stone Newspaper Cuttings, 5, p. 29.

area.[3] Harrison was a man very much like Stone, deeply curious about both new and old things and with a clear view about how he wanted things done. When he arrived in Birmingham as a science teacher in 1880, he had only recently taken up photography. The Birmingham Photographic Society, founded in mid-1857, had by this time folded. In its earliest years it had recruited some thirty members, but attendance at meetings had been thin and its first exhibition of 600 photographs at the Hen and Chickens Hotel in New Street had attracted only a handful of visitors. [4] By 1884, Harrison had secured the re-establishment of the BPS, with himself as vice-president. With the convenience of new hand-held cameras, photography was growing in popularity and, within a few years, the BPS had recruited 200 members. In its earliest incarnation the BPS had confined its discussions to technical matters – dry and wet processes, a newly-invented solar camera and so on – but now at meetings, and in the photographic press, Harrison began to talk about something very different. The camera, he argued, could be a vital tool of preservation – a way of recording for future generations old buildings in danger of disappearing.

Surprisingly Stone did not join the BPS, though he corresponded with Harrison. He learned of Harrison's disappointment that his ambitions were not shared by some of his fellow members of the BPS. In autumn 1889 the two men hatched a plan. Stone invited Harrison to address the Vesey Club, an elitist club made up of wealthy men with an intellectual disposition which met regularly in Sutton Coldfield. Harrison welcomed the opportunity to address a gathering of men with influence and money. The outcome was a declaration of public support, and, in November 1889, Stone's election as president as the BPS. Whilst Harrison was undoubtedly the instigator of record photography in

---

[3] P. James, 'Evolution of the Photographic Record and Survey Movement c. 1890-1910', *History of Photography*, Vol. 12, (3), (1988), pp. 205-218. Also see, E. Edwards, P. James and M. Barnes, (eds.), *A Record of England: Sir Benjamin Stone and the National Photographic Record Association*, (2006), and E. Edwards, *The Camera as Historian: Amateur Photographers and Historical Imagination 1885-1918*, (2012).
[4] *BDG,* 21 September, 28 September 1857, 7 June, 3 November 1858, 7 December 1861; *Birmingham Journal,* 4 June 1859, 3 November 1860.

Birmingham and its environs, he found in Stone an influential ally who had the clout and determination to push things forward.[5]

At a special meeting of the BPS at the Grand Hotel in Birmingham in December 1889, Harrison and Stone unveiled their plans for a photographic survey of Warwickshire. Harrison read a paper setting out how the operation would be carried out, and Stone played his part by lightening the mood with his some remarks about the 'interesting pictures' that could be taken of 'great and historic' trees. There was opposition to the new move. For some members of the BPS, it seemed as if they were being denied their freedom to use their cameras as they chose. At a dinner of the BPS in April 1890, Stone assured his critics that the survey 'should be conducted not as dry matter-of-fact business but as a matter of sentiment.' 'Difficulties had been suggested', he continued, 'but he never believed in difficulties'. It was, Stone believed, only a question of finding 'the right men', and one month later he announced that a separate committee, made up of representatives from photographic societies from across Warwickshire, would be established. In June 1890, the ten members of this new committee, with Stone at the helm, met for the first time. [6]

Stone was excited by what lay ahead. 'The survey', he declared, 'would include photographs of all buildings which were likely to be pulled down or repaired, photographs of geological strata, of old manuscripts and any other objects of artistic, literary or scientific interest.' And, as he eagerly pointed out, they were taking photographs of places that Shakespeare might have known. For sure, these amateur photographers were engaged in work which would be 'of enormous value to posterity'. To ensure this great cause of record photography received the publicity it deserved, an exhibition was put on at the Temperance Hall in December 1890. Many of the photographs on display had been commissioned by Stone twenty or more years earlier. But photographs of such places as the house where the famous Lunar Society met, which had been threatened by demolition, and of Castle Bromwich Hall, which had

---

[5] *BDP*, 15 October 1889; *Photographic Societies Reporter*, 31 October 1889.
[6] *BDP,* 12 December 1889, 22 April, 23 May, 14 June 1890.

been damaged by fire, made very clear the value of the mission Stone had embarked on.[7]

With Stone and Harrison as president and vice-president respectively and its own committee and its own subscription, the Warwickshire Photographic Survey was working in earnest by the summer of 1891. These were true amateurs at work - no one was paid, the results weren't always up to scratch, there was more subjectivity than Harrison really wanted. By the autumn 'some hundreds' of photographs had been taken; by the early months of 1892 the survey was declared to have 'settled into a systematic groove' with its tally amounting to 681 photographs. To prevent fading, members were instructed that only prints developed in platinum or carbon and on bromide paper would be accepted. In May 1892 the WPS, now proudly claiming over 1000 photographs, arranged an exhibition. In total 609 pictures went on display, each with titles handwritten by Stone's daughter Dora. Harrison contributed 200 photographs and the Vesey Club stalwart E. C. Middleton 167, with Stone drawing mostly on old favourites from his collection. One unnamed lady, viewing the exhibition in the half hour before catching her train to Warwick, declared that the pictures 'should be seen to be enjoyed and no true lover of the county could begrudge an afternoon spent in viewing such gems as the photographs are'. Harrison and Middleton did indeed have photographic talent, but this was less evident in pictures taken by their colleagues that featured hats and umbrellas. 'Some of them - which it would be unkind to specify - will need to be replaced as soon as may be by better ones', one local newspaper commented. All of the photographs deemed worthy of preservation were presented to the Free Libraries Committee. In October 1893, another 335 photographs, all in albums, joined the 995 already presented. Though Stone talked up what had been accomplished– it was 'absolutely the first attempt that had been made to form a collection of historical records by means of photography'–it was a real achievement and the WPS had certainly been more successful than similar ventures in other parts of the country.[8]

---

[7] *BDP,* 23 May, 17 December 1890.
[8] *BDP*, 18 September 1891, 7 March, 14 May 1892, 7 October, 11 October 1893; *Leamington Spa Courier,* 21 May, 10 September 1892.

Stone grew more ambitious. Whilst Harrison and his band of fifty local photographers were left to get on with taking pictures in Warwickshire, he adjusted his horizons.   Instead of buying photographs or employing photographers when he disappeared on his foreign travels, Stone took his own hand-held camera.[9] At an exhibition in February 1893, 300 photographs taken by the WPS were eclipsed by a selection taken by Stone in Switzerland the previous autumn; in March 1893 an audience in Nechells 'frequently applauded' pictures Stone took during his exploration of Japan two years earlier; and in December 1894 the BPA displayed the results of Stone's photographic exploits earlier in the year in South Africa. [10]

It was Stone's election as an MP in 1895 that changed his fortunes as a photographer. The London press were intrigued, and entertained, by a parliamentarian whose main contribution to political life appeared to be lining up his colleagues on the terrace of the House of Commons to take their pictures. His colleagues, notably Chamberlain, encouraged him to pursue his hobby. Within a few years of his election the Member for East Birmingham was a household name.

---

[9] *Worcester Journal,* 21 March 1896, for a lecture, accompanied by 150 lantern slides, by J. H. Pickard on his contribution to the WPS.
[10] *BDP*, 20 February, 7 March 1893, 5 December 1894.

6 Round the World

Foreign travel held immense appeal for Stone. He left Britain on no fewer than twenty nine occasions; indeed during the two decades between 1890 and 1910 there were only three years when he did not venture abroad. He was accompanied on these expeditions - which lasted between one and three months - by male friends, notably by his brother-in-law and business partner Frederick Knight, or by his children. Jane was content to remain at home, and limited her travelling to Yorkshire and North Wales. With his well-stocked library, Stone could read about the geology, botany, customs and history of other countries; but he wanted to learn about these things at first hand and, of course, take photographs and bring home plants and rocks. His favourite destination was Norway, which he first visited in 1864 and returned to in 1875, 1882, 1890 and 1895. Inevitably he grew more ambitious, culminating in a voyage around the world in 1891 and a 1000 mile trip up the Amazon in 1893.

Travelling abroad was a taxing undertaking for the Victorian gentleman. It could take days to reach a destination. There were numerous stories of flea-ridden beds, very basic lavatories, small breakfasts and the absence of tea. Stone valued his comforts, and dealt with these difficulties when he was travelling in Europe by staying in the best hotels which provided him with the meals he ate at home. That he was able to travel and at the same time enjoy the comforts of home was due to Thomas Cook (1808-1892), who began organising visits for the affluent to the Continent and the Near-East in the 1860s. During this decade Stone took part in four conducted tours, including, at a cost of 130 guineas, a three month tour of Egypt and the Holy Land by train, steamer and carriage in the first part of 1869. Cook arranged the Channel crossings, the first class rail travel, the steamers 'with good sleeping accommodation' and the comfortable hotels, and often travelled with his clients or sent an assistant. For travellers, Stone wrote, Cook's arrangements 'at once relieves them from endless petty annoyances and from the dread of prospective troubles'. [1]

During a holiday in Spain in summer 1872 Stone penned seventeen letters for the Tory daily, the *Birmingham Daily Gazette*. Well received by the paper's readers, these letters duly appeared the following year as *A Tour with Cook Through Spain*. Stone was an observant man and had a talent for descriptive writing, and his book is something of a page-turner. He liked most of the people he encountered, including his 'light-hearted and merry' guide during a solitary ramble to collect wild flowers outside Cordoba who 'sings bits of songs and amuses me with all kinds of comical expressions'. Of the different cities he visited, Barcelona, with its medieval buildings, was 'by far...the handsomest one in Spain'. He sampled different wines, and found the coffee 'really a delicious beverage'. In Madrid he spent an evening at the bull ring, and, though taken by the colour and the excitement of the people, was horrified by the slaughter of four bulls and, particularly, of forty-two horses:

The cruelty of the "sport" appears tenfold greater when you know that the poor horses are blindfolded and have no means of escape or defence ... No words can describe the sickening feeling which these scenes of barbarous cruelty produce. Some of our party who, like ourselves, are looking upon such scenes for the first time, groan aloud in their terrible excitement. Indeed what expressions can one use when witnessing such a spectacle! Horses trailing their own entrails round the ring; the bull maddened with pain, snorting and covered with blood; the people shouting and making strange noises and the band lustily playing popular tunes.

The party stayed at fine hotels, including the 'most comfortable' Grand Hotel de Paris in Madrid and the Washington Irving Hotel in Granada. Less enjoyable was the railway travel; these journeys often began or ended during the night and were 'tedious', the party feeling 'imprisoned' as they 'endure(d) the over-taxed tempers of each other...' and 'the incessant smoking and keen draughts from open windows...' On occasions Stone and his companions had no alternative but to take to 'the dreaded roads',

---

[1] J. B. Stone, *A Tour With Cook Through Spain*, (1873), p. v; Library of Birmingham, Sir J. B. Stone Newspaper Cuttings, 1, p. 24, for Cook's brochure for his tours to Egypt and the Holy Land.

some of them mountainous, 'over which we are dragged violently by the powerful team of mules'. At least they were spared being the victims of robbery. Another party travelling on a train from Barcelona to Perpignan in France were forced to lie face down by men armed with knives and relieved of their cash, watches and jewellery, leading Stone to conclude that 'careful arrangements should be made to travel as much as possible by daylight'.[2]

Stone had found his tour of Spain fascinating but uncomfortable and exhausting. He did not return for many years, and opted instead for holidays with his male companions in places which he believed would improve his health–such as Norway and Sweden in 1875 and Switzerland in 1881. It was a three-month family expedition to Norway in 1882 that prompted him to write his second travel book. *Children in Norway* (1884) is very much an educational text in which the fjords, glaciers, rare plants, birds of prey, reindeer and musk ox to be observed on a journey from Christiania to the mountain range of Dovrefjell in central Norway are described. Stone wrote as a kindly father patiently answering his children's questions and encouraging them to collect botanical specimens. When asked if his children took an interest in botany, Stone replied, 'Certainly they do, and, as they have quick and accurate observation, they readily recognize a new plant or moss and will distinguish the special features by which they may be known another time'. They had, he went on, derived 'much satisfaction' from discovering a rare moss. On the many days that it rained, the children devoted themselves to drying, measuring and arranging their botanical specimens and sketching the views. Fortunately their hosts always remembered to lay on for them an English tea. Stone might, one newspaper noted, 'have given a far better record of his experiences'. For all its good intentions, the book is, in truth, hardly gripping. Stone probably derived more pleasure from writing it than any children, including his own, did from reading it. When a Liberal newspaper learned that Stone had

---

[2] J. B. Stone, *A Tour With Cook Through Spain*, pp. 22, 28, 59, 64-66, 77, 134, 186, 276. For a review of the book see the *Figaro*, 20 August 1873. See *The Times*, 10 May 1872, for a letter from Stone describing the robbery on the train.

sent a copy to Queen Victoria, it sardonically observed that this was
'a Tory way of currying royal favour'. [3]

Thomas Cook had first offered a voyage around the world in
1872-1873; Richard Tangye of the Cornwall engineering works was
one of the first Birmingham men to avail himself of the
opportunity. Stone was not tempted at all by Cook's American
expeditions, but was strongly attracted to a world tour. There was a
strangeness to countries such as Malaysia and Japan that he had a
deep desire to experience. He also believed that a long ocean
voyage would do wonders for his health. Having shaken off 'a
severe chill', he left England on 24 January 1891 and, in the first
few weeks, contentedly visited places he was already familiar with; in
Naples, he once again contemplated Vesuvius 'whose grandeur
increases in estimation the more you gaze upon it'. The ship
proceeded through the Suez Canal and across the Indian Ocean to
Ceylon, 'a moving picture' and, geologically, a real treat for Stone.
In March, Penang, a British colony in Malaysia, was reached, and
there Stone discovered 'chopsticks in incessant operation, evening
siestas on the ground...rich Hindustanees with flowing robes and
bright turbans...tempting slices of pineapple...disgusting fish of
strange forms'. In mid-April, after briefly calling at Canton in China,
'a hive of busy activity', the ship reached Nagasaki on the east coast
of Japan. The party remained in Japan for three months, and Stone
was delighted by all that he saw. He met up with the engineer and
photographer W. K. Burton (1856-1899) and spent time studying–
and photographing–the dramatic effects on the landscape of the
eruption of the Bandai-San volcano three years earlier. He was
impressed by flowers that decorated tea houses and hotels and by
the rickshaw men, much more obliging he thought that the cabbies
of Birmingham. He even sampled raw fish which 'was really nice
but I did not eat much'. Some of the children were too inquisitive
for Stone's liking and the fleas particularly annoyed him, leading
him to sew up the bottom of his night dress. From Japan, Stone
sailed across the Pacific to Canada where he met his second son
Norman. Together they explored the 'majestic and wonderful'
scenery of the country before returning home across the Atlantic.
During this voyage Stone had sent home negatives taken on his

[3] J. B. Stone, *Children in Norway* (1884), pp. 27, 168; *Graphic*, 22
March 1884.

small Kodak No. 2 camera, plant specimens and a series of vivid letters. He also published, with Burton, an account of his three months in Japan, *On The Great Highway* (1892). [4]

Sharing his knowledge and discovering new things with like-minded men gave Stone great pleasure. With members of the Vesey Club, he visited Norway in summer 1890 and Switzerland and Italy in summer 1892. These were not tours organized by Cook, but arranged by Stone in association with the company. The cost of the exploration of the fjords and coastal towns of Norway was £30 for 23 days, with the party residing on their steamer, the *St. Rognauld*. Experts within the Club led investigations into the geology and flora of the country. On their return an exhibition was put on featuring Stone's photographs and various geological and botanical specimens that had been brought back. Stone himself returned with 'well nigh a cartload' of mosses. For their visit to Switzerland and Italy, these inquiring men travelled by night train and steamer from London to Lausanne and, staying in agreeable hotels, were able to inspect Lake Geneva, attempt to climb the Matterhorn and linger for a week in Laveno in Lombardy. [5]

The voyage around the world certainly did not sate Stone's appetite for exotic travel. It only made him want more. In March 1893 this intrepid man embarked on another ambitious expedition. Leaving Southampton on the packet steamer *Trent*, he sailed for Pernambuco on the coast of north-east Brazil and then proceeded to Ceara, where he joined a British eclipse expedition. On 16 April 1893, 'in perfectly clear weather' Stone was able to photograph a total eclipse of the sun. He next joined a smaller party on a journey of almost one thousand miles up the Amazon, taking with him his two hand-held camera and one thousand whole plate films.[6] It was six months before he returned home, as he explored parts of

---

[4] *BDP*, 8 January 1891; 'Round the World' Letters, pp. 8, 21, 35-6, 66, 80, 156 in the possession of the Stone family; Library of Birmingham, Sir J. B. Stone Newspaper Cuttings, 2, p. 6. Durham University Library is the only library in the UK to hold a copy of *On The Great Highway*.

[5] *Birmingham Mercury,* 30 December 1890; Library of Birmingham, Sir J. B. Stone Newspaper Cuttings, 35, pp. 114, 121; Sutton Coldfield Library, 'Vesey Club excursion to Switzerland, June 1892'

[6] *BDP,* 27 March, 6 February 1893; *The Times,* 17 April 1893; *Daily Graphic,* 28 June 1893; *Dover Express,* 21 April 1893; *Burnley Express,* 26 August 1893.

Central America and the Caribbean, ensuring that the itinerary included a visit to the famous asphalt Pitch Lake in Trinidad. Stone had managed to survive, and so, in March 1894, departed for South Africa on the steamer *Norham Castle*. He was accompanied by his daughter Ethel, and travelled initially by railway and then by open wagon through 'some of the more unknown parts of Zululand, Swaziland and other districts which have in recent years been brought under British influence'. He was able to inspect interesting geological features and take photographs of Zulus and the 'fine' residences of the white population. These photographs, he declared on his return, were 'of historical interest–so much as until now the Zulus had been untainted... [They] were the finest of savage races in the world'. [7]

Whilst he was fit and well, Stone had no intention of giving up his travelling. At the offices of P&O in Northumberland Avenue and at those of Thomas Cook & Sons, in Ludgate Circus he remained a very familiar face. In spring 1895, over twenty years since his last visit, Stone went back to Egypt and the Holy Land, and that autumn spent a month in Norway. On the first of these expeditions, he arrived at Suez and, after a night at the comfy Suez Hotel, travelled by train to Cairo. He visited the mosques and bazaars before travelling by carriage to the Pyramids. Like other British travellers, he was able to rely on the employees of Cook & Sons in Egypt to make arrangements for him. 'I will say that in Egypt and Syria', Richard Tangye wrote, 'the name of "Cook" is the talisman which solves all difficulties and robs travelling of nearly all its inconveniences'. [8]

In summer 1897, Stone returned to Italy, repeating the trip the following year. Stone was never bored by Italy, but his desire to visit new places had not diminished. With his son Oscar, he spent a month in Tunisia in 1904. The two men set up camp in Tunis but travelled 'through gorges and over mountains, going among the tribes and securing pictures which no one had hitherto succeeded in getting'. At Biskra, on the edge of the Sahara, Stone reflected that, though the hotel met his requirements and 'the garden courtyards are full of attractive delights', a long stay could not be

---

[7] *BDP*, 6 March, 3 October, 12 October 1894.
[8] R. Tangye, *Reminiscences of Travel in Australia, America and Egypt*, (1884), p. 241.

recommended for 'carriages are dear, the food is indifferent, the open drains around many houses are offensive and there are many petty annoyances'. At Sidi Okba, in the Sahara itself, he noticed that women were 'scrupulously withdrawn from all observation'. Stone discovered that people in Tunisia were not as eager as those in Britain to let him take their pictures, but still managed to return with 300 new plates. Stone might have been portly and in his mid-sixties, but his days of restless – one might almost say obsessive - travelling were still not at an end.[9]

---

[9] Library of Birmingham, Stone's handwritten notes for exhibitions of his photographs.

7 The Photographer-MP

'There was', Stone observed in December 1895, 'no one in Parliament at the present moment with whom he was in more accord than Mr Chamberlain'. Six months earlier, with 'their opponents hav(ing) disappeared' and therefore able to avoid the strains and anxieties of a contest, Stone had accepted an invitation to succeed Henry Matthews as MP for East Birmingham. 'He considered he was returned as a member who would watch over the interests of the industrial classes', Stone declared at the celebrations that marked his election. 'The eastern division was essentially a working class constituency and matters connected with trade and the comforts of domestic life would more especially have his devoted attention'.[1] Twenty years earlier, Stone had certainly not viewed Chamberlain with feelings of admiration and awe. But things had changed significantly since Stone had challenged Chamberlain's dominance of the town council in those distant days.

In 1886, the Liberals were ruptured by Gladstone's conversion to the cause of a separate legislature for Ireland. Chamberlain objected in principle, advocating instead wider powers of local government; but also saw in Gladstone's scheme the trumping of his own cherished radical causes and a consequent diminution in his standing. He became the most important Liberal opponent of Irish Home Rule. An attempt in early 1887 at the Round Table Conference in London to bring about a Liberal reunion ended–in spite of one Liberal sporting Joe's favourite flower, the orchid–in frustrating failure. In Birmingham, though some continued to urge reconciliation, it came down to the difficult choice for the Liberals of choosing between Gladstone and Chamberlain. For some, such as the BLA's arch-political fixer Francis Schnadhorst, loyalty to Gladstone proved too strong to break. Ever the political opportunist, Stone watched these events with considerable interest. Very early on he saw, in co-operation with Chamberlain and his

---

[1] *BDP*, 5 December 1894, 11 December, 18 December 1895; Sir J. B. Stone Collection of Newspaper Cuttings, 6, p. 26 for a letter expressing disapproval at Stone's return from 'Disgusted'. Chamberlain had been appointed Colonial Secretary in July 1895, and had immediately begun to emphasize the economic benefits of imperialism.

allies, the opportunity for the Conservative cause to make real progress in Birmingham.[2]

The new alliance soon yielded a most satisfactory result. For the first time in forty years a Conservative MP was returned in Birmingham. He was Henry Matthews (1826-1913), who, though a celebrated barrister was unexpectedly appointed Home Secretary. For Stone it was a turning point. At a garden party at The Grange in July 1886, he declared that 'the old landmarks which had divided the parties were being swept away and he was glad of it ... [but] if the Conservative Party was to be successful, it must be recruited from the ranks of their opponents and, now that many of those opponents were on their side, let an effort be made to keep them'. Matthews, cultured, engaging, witty but shy, gave Stone full credit for his success, revealing that he 'probably would have turned tail. Mr Stone, however, took him by the scruff of his neck and brought him up to scratch'.[3] For Chamberlain's supporters in Birmingham a Conservative MP in the eastern division was accepted only through gritted teeth. The strains between the two sides that made up the new Unionist alliance were more real than Stone wanted to accept.

A friendship which lasted for the rest of their lives developed between Stone and Matthews. It was a relationship based on far more than shared political views, and, whenever Matthews visited Birmingham either privately or to address his constituents, he was always a welcome guest at The Grange. Despite Stone's best efforts, relations between the Conservatives and Liberal Unionists in Birmingham remained uneasy. With the death of John Bright in March 1889, a dispute arose over whether a Conservative or a Liberal Unionist candidate would claim the vacancy in Central Birmingham. At the heart of the disagreement was a claim by the Conservatives that Chamberlain had failed to honour a promise made at a private dinner that the seat would go to Lord Randolph Churchill. When Churchill, behind the scenes in London, was talked out of putting himself forward, many Conservatives in

---

[2] G. Searle, *A New England? Peace and War 1886-1918*, (2004), pp. 149-162; I. Cawood, *The Liberal Unionist Party: A History*, (2012), pp. 77-105; P. Marsh, *Joseph Chamberlain*, pp. 238-244, 260, 300.

[3] *BDP*, 26 July 1892. In the six other constituencies in Birmingham Liberal Unionist MPs were elected.

Birmingham were left feeling very sore. What prompted the Liberal Unionists to dig their heels in was their very promising canvass returns, and their candidate John Albert Bright was indeed returned, by a good margin, in April 1889. Unlike some of his fellow Conservatives, who sat on their hands, Stone publicly supported Bright during the campaign.[4]

Stone continued to seek to reduce the political temperature. He spoke of the 'sacrifices' of the Liberal Unionists and made clear that he 'was not prepared to say to them in Birmingham that their seats were weak and the Conservatives had a right to them'. He urged his colleagues not to provoke each other. 'It would be well if friends on both sides would be less acrimonious in their remarks', he observed before Matthews delivered his annual speech in his constituency in October 1889, 'and not cause irritation on both sides. It was plainly their duty to cement the friendship'. Unfortunately for Stone, cementing the friendship was the last thing on the minds of many of the eighteen delegates who gathered at a conference proposed by Chamberlain at the Queen's Hotel in Birmingham the following month. Stone listened to the speeches, hoping that 'some friendly arrangement ... of a private nature' might result in Bright standing down but, at the end of the first day, announcing that 'they had not seen a glimmer of light'. A second day of wrangling, with four of the delegates deciding it wasn't worth turning up, resulted in a battered Stone, who by now 'viewed the condition of things in a worse light than before', proposing that the national leaders of both parties be asked to resolve the differences over parliamentary candidates in Birmingham.[5]

It took a year to get an answer, but it was the answer the Liberal Unionists wanted. From this point on Birmingham would be a stronghold of Liberal Unionism. Though many Birmingham Conservatives made plain their unhappiness with developments, Stone, refreshing himself with long holidays, continued to uphold the compact with the Liberal Unionists. In East Birmingham, he reported, relations between the two sides were 'cordial and sincere' and, at a meeting in Nechells, declared that they should 'watch very carefully that they were in sympathy with the large numbers of

---

[4] *BDP*, 5 April, 6 April, 12 April 1889; P. Marsh, *Joseph Chamberlain*, pp. 311, 315-316.
[5] *BDP*, 17 October, 5 November, 18 November 1889.

working men in the ward'. With Matthews in his mid-sixties and also facing much press criticism for his performance as Home Secretary, talk began to turn to Stone as the next MP.[6]

The Gladstonian Liberals, however, were determined not go quietly. When Chamberlain spoke in East Birmingham in January 1891, Stone, as chairman, was interrupted with cries of 'sit down' and 'turn him out' before he had the chance to announce that he 'extended to Mr Chamberlain the hand of friendship as warm and sincere as he was sincere in opposing him in days gone by'. That November a Gladstonian Liberal was elected in Saltley, the Unionist candidate George Coghill 'heartlessly betrayed by many Conservatives ...' Stone struggled to understand why bitter feelings continued to damage the Unionist cause. He declared himself 'amazed to think that because someone was personally annoyed, he should make it a party question.'[7]

The East Birmingham Unionists faced a significant challenge in the general election of July 1892. Henry Matthews was a much lambasted Home Secretary. He was blamed for the way the police handled 'Bloody Sunday' in November 1889, when two men were killed during protests in Trafalgar Square, and for the reprieve of only the younger of two brothers convicted of murdering their violent father in 1890. Stone manfully defended Matthews, maintaining that 'while there had been an undercurrent of dissatisfaction in certain quarters, he had proved himself to be a strong Home Secretary and a good candidate'. For more than a year the Gladstonian candidate H. S. Fulford had been nursing the constituency. Naturally he stressed the importance of Irish Home Rule, but he was a brewer and this - helpfully for Matthews - led to the emergence of a temperance advocate in Liberal colours, D. Shilton Collins. Though Fulford's supporters managed to get one of Collins' sandwich board men drunk and, much to Stone's chagrin, pasted their posters over those of the Unionists, they could not counter the impact of a big speech in the constituency by Chamberlain followed by the arrival of 400 Unionist workers, sporting red, white and blue. Matthews was returned with a majority of 2209.[8] Stone also got his reward. It had taken twenty

[6] *BDP*, 15 January, 20 February, 20 November, 16 December 1890.
[7] *BDP*, 16 January, 30 November 1891, 1 March 1892.
[8] *BDP*, 13 January, 30 June, 1 July 1892; *BDG*, 4 July, 14 July 1892.

five years for him to see his efforts on behalf of the Conservative cause in Birmingham bear fruit. But at last his political views held sway in his own town. In August 1892, he received a letter from his party leader Salisbury, informing him that he was to receive a knighthood; and, at Buckingham Palace, on 2 December 1892, this great champion of the constitution proudly knelt before his monarch.[9]

* * * *

A strong ambition to enter the House of Commons could not be said to have ever gripped Stone. He certainly ruled out putting himself through a bruising election campaign against the powerful BLA in the 1870s and 1880s, and it was only in the early 1890s, as the local political situation began to change, that his views about being a parliamentary candidate altered. Stone was more than happy to have Matthews as the Unionist MP for East Birmingham, but, when his friend decided to retire and there appeared no prospect of a challenge from the Liberals, he agreed that his name could go forward. By this time Stone had acquired more experience in local government, securing the locally-prestigious role as the first mayor of Sutton Coldfield. This market town of about 8000 inhabitants had replaced its warden and society with an elected corporation of eighteen councillors and six aldermen. The first task of these men, many of them manufacturers and businessmen who had recently arrived in the town, was the election, from amongst themselves, of a mayor.

Returned unopposed as one of the councillors for the Wylde Green ward, Stone had ambitions to be mayor. He discovered that Joseph Ansell, a member of the Aston brewing family and an old school friend, also had his eye on the post. A deal was done: Ansell nominated Stone as mayor and Stone nominated Ansell as his deputy. Though Stone regretted 'the apparent conflict', Ansell, in spite of being an active Liberal, proved to be very loyal to Stone, recognising in him 'exceptional ability...on questions of finance'. 'Under his regime', Ansell declared of the mayor, 'he did not think

---

[9] Library of Birmingham, Sir Benjamin Stone, Copies of Illuminated and Other Addresses, 1869-1907, Salisbury to Stone, 15 August 1892; Library of Birmingham, Sir J. B. Stone Newspaper Cuttings, 2, p. 16.

there was much fear of the rates being increased.' When, in October 1887, Stone declined nomination, it was Ansell who led the chorus to change his mind. 'They had', he gushed, 'seen in the actions of Mr Stone the firmness and diplomacy of a Talleyrand combined with the gentleness of a Chesterfield...' The new council met each month to hear reports from committees dealing with such matters as finance, public health, the fire brigade and Sutton Park. Offered a mayor's robe, Stone declared that 'if it should add to the dignity of the town (laughter), he should only be too glad to wear it'. He was certainly glad to wear the new eighteen carat gold mayoral chain, decorated with symbols associated with the town's Tudor patrons, acquired in June 1887.[10]

During the four years he served as mayor Stone, true to his reputation, was ever watchful with regard to finances. He resisted increasing the rates, preferring to borrow prudently from the Local Government Board for such projects as improving the roads and sewers. In October 1887, he secured a halving (from £610 to £300) of Sutton's contribution to the running costs of Saltley police station and Aston magistrates' room; one year later Sutton acquired its own police station and police court. [11]

At the heart of Stone's deeply-held belief in his country's constitutional heritage was his reverence for the monarchy. He ensured that the celebrations for the Golden Jubilee in June 1887 would be truly memorable for the people of Sutton Coldfield. The festivities lasted for a week. Jubilee medals and brooches were manufactured for the boys and girls of the town, and, on Jubilee Day itself (21 June), there was a church service and a procession, and, in Sutton Park, sports, maypole dancing, bell-ringing, dinner for the elderly and the planting of two oak trees in the park by Stone and his wife, all rounded off by the launching of rockets into the night sky. So enjoyable did Stone find all this merrymaking that, a few weeks later, the park keepers and boatmen of Sutton Park were rewarded with their own tea in the park and further

---

[10] *BDP*, 25 March, 31 March ,10 April, 12 June, 18 November 1886, 16 June, 11 October, 31 October, 10 November 1887. Talleyrand (1754-1838) was a long-serving French diplomat; Lord Chesterfield (1694-1773) was a man known for his *bons mots*.
[11] *BDP*, 27 May, 3 June 1886, 6 October, 8 December 1887, 4 May, 26 September 1888.

demonstrations of maypole dancing and dumb bell lifting by local girls and boys. That December four of these girls accompanied Stone to Windsor Castle where he presented the Queen with an album of photographs he had taken of the celebrations. The Jubilee celebrations made a profit of £372, a significant contribution towards the £545 required to meet Stone's ambition of purchasing land and building a dispensary in the town. The rest of the money for the dispensary was obtained by even more maypole dancing in Sutton Park and a series of concerts, the first of which, in December 1887, was attended by 'the largest audience that has perhaps ever been witnessed inside the town hall'. The dispensary, where local people could obtain advice and medicines, opened in February 1889; within two years it had 1332 subscribers who had contributed £212.2s.10d.[12]

By April 1890, Stone was complaining of 'the onerous duties pertaining to public life', and soon afterwards decided not to seek re-election as mayor of Sutton Coldfield. His easy-going, placatory manner had usually helped him get his way in the public offices he held, but he was not without his critics. 'Surely there never was a man in the world so inordinately puffed up with vanity as Mr J. B. Stone of Erdington', a fellow Conservative complained in November 1888. And not everyone shared Stone's delight at maypole dancing; during one discussion about a summer fete, one of his fellow councillors expressed 'the hope that there would be something more pleasurable than mere maypole dancing'. For his work in Sutton Coldfield Stone was presented with those traditional Victorian gifts to public men – an illuminated address and a service of plate.[13]

---

[12] *BDP*, 13 June, 7 July, 8 August, 12 December 1887, 21 March, 16 July, 3 August 1888; *Daily News,* 1 December 1887; Library of Birmingham, Sir J. B. Stone Newspaper Cuttings, 35, p. 76, for the first annual report on the dispensary. The dispensary finally closed in 1948 with the launch of the National Health Service.

[13] *BDP*, 12 November, 14 November 1888, 3 April, 11 November 1890. John A. Bridges was another Conservative who did not admire Stone: *Reminiscences*, pp. 173-184, for his surprise at discovering Stone, at a meeting of the council of the National Union, 'exalted into an important political personage ... were I Prime Minister, I would certainly have one such man as Lord Hugh Cecil on my side...than any number of Sir

A link with Sutton Coldfield that outlasted Stone's mayoralty was the Vesey Club, established in the town in July 1888. Stone had long corresponded with, and invited to The Grange, men who shared his enthusiasms. He became the prime mover in the establishment of a private club 'in which it was sought to assemble the brightest intellects of the neighbourhood.' The famous benefactor of Sutton Coldfield Bishop Vesey (1452-1554) gave his name to this fellowship of forty successful men. Those who were invited to join, at a cost of ten shillings, were men very much like Stone. They had inquiring minds and were self-taught in the fields in which they claimed expertise. Several of the members had made names for themselves: Charles Lapworth (1842-1920), a self-educated geologist who had risen from being a school master to a professor at Mason College, knew as much about the rocks of the midlands as it was possible for any man to know and was awarded prestigious medals for his work; Henry Crosskey (1826-1893), the pastor of the Church of the Messiah, wrote extensively on the glacial geology of Scotland; J. E. Bagnall (1830-1918) worked as a clerk in a pen factory, but was the author such notable works as the *Handbook of Mosses* (1886) and *Flora of Warwickshire* (1890); and S. H. Baker (1824-1909) was a painter known for his water colours of rural scenes. The Vesey Club met monthly, initially at the mayor's cottage in Sutton Park, to discuss matters of a scientific and antiquarian nature. Thus, in the first year, there were papers on fungi, the poetry of Tennyson, meteorology and explosives, at the latter of which there were some demonstrations 'but it is pleasant to add that no lives were lost'. Stone himself often talked about his collections of photographs and fossils and his travels, being greeted at his first meeting after returning from Japan, in October 1891, by cries of 'skoal' and the singing of 'he's a jolly good fellow'. These gentlemen occasionally took themselves off on study visits: a two-day visit to Ludlow and Church Stretton in autumn 1890, including dinner and a room at The Feathers, cost thirty shillings and a one-

Benjamin Stones'. Cecil, elected MP for Greenwich in 1895, was a staunch defender of the Church of England.

day visit to Lincoln by specially-chartered train in summer 1901 cost £16/6d.[14]

* * * *

'Who said Sir Benjamin Stone was a parliamentary failure?', one Birmingham Liberal newspaper observed in 1897. 'Let the caitiff hide his head while there is still time ... It is not that Sir Benjamin Stone has been called to fill the premiership during the temporary absence of Lord Salisbury ... [He] lives, moves and labours on a higher plane...The ruck of constituencies send mere politicians [to Westminster]. East Birmingham has sent a photographer.' In the years after he became an MP Stone's photographic exploits had indeed featured far more frequently in the newspapers than anything he had done in the political sphere. This was because he had, for the most part, been content to observe, rather than participate in, parliamentary proceedings. Stone recorded his impressions of the leading politicians of the day in his diaries. He was impressed by an 'excellent' speech the Leader of the Opposition Sir Henry Campbell Bannerman made in February 1899, less so by the 'halting' reply of the First Lord of the Treasury Arthur Balfour, from whom there was, a few months later, another fumble 'ending in a fiasco & damage to him & the Conservative Party'. Though he certainly did not agree with them, Stone listened, in October 1899, with some understanding to Sir Edward Clarke and Leonard Courtney, the Unionist critics of the war in South Africa and, in January 1900, even recognised 'a powerful attack' on Chamberlain by the Liberal Sir Robert Reid. In December 1900, criticisms of Salisbury and Chamberlain were described as 'acrimonious & personal', and speeches by the Labour men John Burns and Keir Hardie as 'violent'. Occasionally events in the chamber did get on the nerves of the normally placid Stone. The speeches of Irish Nationalist MPs he found 'difficult to distinguish [from] ...what was called treason to king and country'. In April

---

[14] *BDP*, 11 September 1888, 11 February, 13 March, 1 May, 24 September 1890, 22 October 1891, 16 March, 16 August 1892, 20 February 1893, 12 October 1894; Sutton Coldfield Library, Vesey Club, Annual Meeting, 1 June 1889; Library of Birmingham, Sir J. B. Stone Newspaper Cuttings, 32, is devoted to the Vesey Club.

1899, he witnessed 'some stupid voting' on women councillors and, in March 1900, 'pro-Boer irritation'. Stone himself spoke on only four occasions in the 1895-1900 Parliament – two questions (one on a threat to paper manufacturers) and an unsuccessful attempt, in January 1897, to introduce a private members' bill to deal with the possession of stolen property. He did sit on the petroleum committee and presented petitions to restrict the sale of alcohol, but most of his contributions to political debate seem to have taken place in the smoking room.[15]

In East Birmingham in early 1900, Stone defended the war in South Africa. 'He had travelled amongst the Boers', he informed an audience of Conservative supporters in January 1900, 'and he was bound to say that they were a rough, uncultivated and untutored people. They would ... give help to one when travelling the country, although they would not give it with the same heartiness as our own people'. It was, he continued, the 'severe cruelty' towards black Africans of these 'extremely bigoted' people that had in fact caused the war. Stone might have travelled in South Africa, but he had shared the view that, with the outbreak of war in October 1899, an easy victory would ensue. The Boers had in fact outwitted the British in the early months of the war, trapping large numbers of soldiers in Ladysmith, Kimberley and Mafeking. It was, Stone recognised, 'a serious war' and 'disaster – if one could conceive of such a thing – would not only mean the loss of prestige in South Africa but in all parts of our empire'. Advising the officers of the Birmingham Volunteer Battalion, whose 232 men had been equipped by local subscriptions, at a farewell dinner in January 1900, that 'if it were not for the dangers of war...they would have...a very enjoyable time', Stone's old confidence, badly shaken during 'Black Week' in December 1899, began to return. To his great

---

[15] S. Roberts, 'The Photographer-MP: Selections from the Diaries of Sir Benjamin Stone, 1897-1909, *West Midlands Studies*, 18, (1985), pp. 32-38. All quotations from Stone's diaries in this chapter are taken from this essay. Library of Birmingham, Sir J. B. Stone Newspaper Cuttings 5, p. 18. *Bristol Mercury,* 2 December 1898, for a report of a short speech in the city by Stone, 'a pleasant old gentleman ... who is most at home when at Birmingham', which led a fellow speaker to utter 'the astounding, hardly-believable statement that he wished Sir Benjamin had gone on speaking for another hour'.

relief, one by one, the besieged towns were recaptured. Stone himself called at the War Office, in March 1900, to read the reports that Ladysmith had been relieved. 'Streets full & people excited over the war news', he wrote in his diary.[16]

With the annexation of the Transvaal in October 1900, Salisbury sought to capitalise on the patriotic mood by calling an election. Stone had expected a dissolution and, with the Birmingham Liberals a pale shadow of what they once had been, looked forward to not having to trouble his working class electors with speeches and canvassing. East Birmingham was a centre of heavy industry, particularly the manufacture of railway plant and gas making. People in work, and certainly the many out of work, struggled to make ends meet, and the local newspaper spoke of 'poverty, destitution and starvation amidst the most squalid and appalling conditions'. Good houses were 'scarce and dear' and, in 1899, an extension to the gasworks absorbed the only recreation ground in Nechells. Stone declared his 'deep interest' in the question of housing, but for some of his constituents this was not enough. The East Birmingham Labour League wanted to see working men represented by their own class, and, in 1897, secured the return of a gas worker Robert Toller to the city council. Things were beginning to change, but, fortunately for Stone, at a slow pace. With only a fortnight until polling no candidate had emerged to oppose his return, such working class leaders as Richard Bell of the railwaymen and Will Thorne of the gas workers having declined invitations to stand.[17]

Across the Birmingham constituencies it seemed that the Unionists would be unchallenged. Even with their dwindling support, the Liberals could see that this was a deplorable situation. And then, at the eleventh hour, a candidate was found to take on Stone. J.V. Stevens (1852-1925), a Lib-Lab councillor and the leader of the tinplate workers, had impeccable credentials for the job. What he did not have was time, men or money, though Toller's Labour League mobilised and the Liberals were able to call

---

[16] *BDP*, 10 January, 12 January, 20 January, 27 January 1900.

[17] S. Roberts, 'Politics and the Birmingham Working Class: The General Elections of 1900 and 1906 in East Birmingham', *West Midlands Studies*, 15, (1982), pp. 12-21. The discussions of Stone's electoral contests in 1900 and 1906 are based on this essay.

on such wealthy backers as George Cadbury. In the circumstances Stevens fought an impressive campaign. At meeting after meeting he spoke of the urgent need for social reform, calling for old age pensions 'quite free from the taint of pauperism', the extension of the 1897 Work Men's Compensation Act, better houses and cheaper tram fares. Anticipating the Unionist line of attack, his literature was embellished with patriotic colours, but, as the city's only Liberal newspaper observed, Stevens had 'recognised duties waiting the attention other than the singing of Rule Britannia'.

Stone concluded his meetings with a chorus of 'God Save The Queen'. Beyond presenting himself as the choice for the patriotic voter, he had little to say. 'Those who watch... [him] at his election meetings', his opponents sarcastically noted, 'can see that he is simply palpitating with restrained energy of thought and speech'. It was in fact to Chamberlain that Stone looked to see him home. Determined that his stronghold would not be breached, Chamberlain duly appeared on a platform for Stone. The limitations of the Work Men's Compensation Act, he declared, made it 'half a loaf...but sometimes half the loaf was the quickest way to get the whole' and, as for old age pensions, he was 'not dead yet'. It was the decisive moment of the campaign, though Stone was also helped by an out-of-date electoral register and heavy rain on polling day–which added together drastically reduced the turn out - and strong rumours – not denied – that, if he was defeated, 'we will all suffer because he will shut his works down'. This time Stone had had no choice but to stay in the country, but his victory by 2,154 votes went some way towards making restitution for the misery of being a candidate in a contested election.

* * * *

During parliamentary sessions Stone treated himself to the luxurious living offered by the Midland Grand Hotel at St. Pancras, where he enjoyed a fire in his room and admired the gold-leafed wallpaper. He relished the opportunities his new life brought him– evenings at the theatre and at aristocratic soirees and access to almost anywhere he wanted to go with his camera. 'Went to the House of Lords to hear the Queen's Speech', he wrote in February 1898. 'Chats with many members in the Lobby, my photographs being the chief subject of conversation. Many compliments...'

Stone's affability got him a long way with various parliamentary officials and he was able to set up his own dark room and begin work taking photographs of his fellow MPs and of the Houses of Parliament. The photographs of his colleagues were taken on the terrace in early afternoon and quickly developed so that their subjects could inspect and autograph them. Stone's colleagues happily co-operated with his enterprise:

> One member would be photographed, then he would call to another, who, perhaps, was quite a stranger to me, and he in turn would induce someone else and so on. For instance, I should not have obtained the portraits of Mr Michael Davitt if it had not been for the kindness of Mr Chamberlain who, seeing Mr Davitt, asked me if he had been photographed. "I will ask him myself to come", and he did ... Of course, some men are better subjects than others and there was a lack of formality and posing about our proceedings which has given in some cases almost a humorous touch to the portrait. Occasionally, too, a smile would be produced on the face of a member by a remark from a bystander, such as when Mr Jesse Collings was requested "to think of a cow". [18]

Everywhere Stone went in the Palace of Westminster he was the recipient of admiring comments. 'It is comforting', he observed without a hint of irony, 'to know that I could do well as a professional photographer if things went very wrong'. Only one MP – the grumpy Liberal Sir William Harcourt – informed Stone that he was unhappy with the photograph that had been taken of him. It was not only MPs that Stone photographed on the terrace of the House of Commons – there were parliamentary officials and visitors, including the writer Mark Twain and the aviator Louis Bleriot. 'When I saw that photograph, with the Mother of Parliaments in the background and realised my advancing years', Twain later observed, 'I said to myself, "Here are two noble monuments of antiquity – two shining examples of the survival of the fittest"'. [19]

---

[18] Quoted in B. Jay, *Customs and Faces,* n.p; Stone was hardly likely to have known the Irish Nationalist Davitt, first elected an MP whilst a prisoner.

[19] Quoted in Jay, *Customs and Faces* n.p; *Evening Telegraph,* 11 May 1910. Mark Twain was the pseudonym of Samuel L. Clemens.

In November 1897 Stone presented one hundred parliamentary portraits, as well as another hundred pictures of the architectural features of the Houses of Parliament, to the British Museum. As ever keen for his pictures to be seen, he arranged for a selection of photographs of MPs to be exhibited at the Royal Photographic Society in March 1900. His own favourites were to adorn the walls of a corridor in the House of Commons until the Second World War. These parliamentary pictures could also be perused in a two volume collection of Stone's photographs brought out by Cassell & Co. in 1906. The first of these volumes depicts the rural customs that Stone was keen to see preserved; but it is the second volume of ninety six pictures– depicting, amongst other things, Balfour, Chamberlain, Davitt, MPs drinking tea on the terrace and Stone's favourite haunt, the smoking room – that has proved to be of most enduring interest.[20]

To the cab drivers of London Stone became a familiar figure as he lugged his weighty camera and tripod around. It fact it was his assistant Mercer who did most of lugging, but not always without mishap: the camera took twenty minutes to set up and disassemble and one day in April 1899 its legs were left behind in Trafalgar Square. Posterity, Stone was sure, would recognise him as an important chronicler of his age. In May 1898 he secured permission to photograph Gladstone's lying-in-state in Westminster Hall – taken in early morning light with a ray of sunlight falling across the coffin, the published photograph was much-praised. In January 1901, on an overcast day, he took six photographs of the proclaiming of Edward VII as king at St. James Palace. 'Good records, bad photographs', he recorded in his diary. In October 1902 he took photographs of the new king's procession through the City of London. 'Had seats erected for photographing the procession, he noted in his diary. Took about fifty plates. Excellent position and fine views'.

In all this excitement Stone had not forgotten his quest to make photographic records of historical documents and objects. In August 1899, he took a large number of photographs of medieval charters in the possession of the City of London. He also managed

---

[20] *The Times*, 9 March 1900; *Cheltenham Chronicle*, 10 February 1906; *Gloucester Citizen*, 17 January 1906; *Dundee Courier*, 1 November 1909.

to scour the Vatican archives that year, triumphantly announcing that he had found, and photographed, a petition to Pope Clement VI from Edward III and a love letter from Henry VIII to Anne Boleyn. In January and April 1900, Stone was able to take 'many beautiful pictures' of the exterior and interior of Windsor Castle as well as of various precious objects in the library. The following year he secured permission to take photographs in the Tower of London, including of the Crown Jewels, and to roam through Hatfield House with his camera, where, disappointingly, he was not offered any lunch.[21]

During all of his photographic forays in London and beyond Stone took a large number of pictures. In some weeks his tally reached almost one hundred pictures; he was 'rarely...seen without a bundle of his latest developments tucked beneath his arm'. It is clear that he invested a significant part of his personal wealth in his great interest. But what was he to do with all of these photographs? Stone, of course, as always, had a plan. He arranged with Sir Edward Maunde Thompson (1840-1929) that they would be deposited in the British Museum. And not just his photographs. They would be joined by the work of other photographers who shared Stone's vision of creating a pictorial record of English history. Launched at Stone's London hotel in July 1897, with himself as president, the National Photographic Record Association sought to bring together photographic societies, individual professional and amateur photographers and collectors in a huge national effort to record for posterity the ancient buildings and customs of England. It was in effect a considerably more ambitious version of the Warwickshire Photographic Society. This time Harrison was not involved, but Stone used his connections to recruit 'an influential council', which included representatives from the Royal Society, the Society of Antiquaries and the Society for the Protection of Ancient Buildings. With an annual subscription of ten shillings, the NPRA attracted, for the most part, middle class amateurs. There were also critics, who rehearsed the complaints that Stone had heard years before about centralisation. 'What use

---

[21] *The Times*, 12 August 1899, 9 March 1900; *Freeman's Journal,* 10 February, 24 March 1899.

will these local prints be to the future local historian if they are buried away in London?' one Manchester photographer enquired.[22]

Intentionally the NPRA was launched in the year of the Golden Jubilee. There could be no better time, Stone reasoned, than to launch a celebration of national identity. Elizabeth Edwards, Peter James and Martin Barnes, in some very interesting observations, have noted that Stone's contributions to the NPRA were imbued with his deep conservatism. His desire to take photographs of manor houses and churches, they suggest, as well as of the stocks and whipping posts by which the law was enforced, indicate his concern for social hierarchies. Whilst they recognise – for example, in a 'magnificent' photograph of the yew trees in Painswick churchyard – that Stone did sometimes achieve high photographic standards, they point out that, on at least one occasion, he photographed his umbrella as well as the building and report 'the poor results of many of his efforts'. Several other NPRA members, notably the secretary George Scamell, who travelled around Hertfordshire and Essex on his bicycle taking photographs of churches, achieved better results than Stone.[23]

Stone emphasised that the technical merit of a photograph was 'of secondary importance as compared with the facts which it records'. He insisted that there was to be no retouching of photographs and that-to record detail – they should be whole-plate and – to ensure they did not deteriorate-platinum or carbon prints. By October 1900, the NPRA had accumulated 1,084 pictures, and by May 1905 3,504. Stone had been constantly on the move. A few examples will suffice: in May 1901 he was in Helstone in Cornwall to take photographs of a centuries old festival called 'the Furry'; in May 1902 he enjoyed 'a right royal reception' in Corby in Northamptonshire being 'chaired round the village, headed by the

---

[22] Quoted in Edwards, James and Barnes (eds.), *A Record of England*, p. 23; *Daily News*, 15 April, 1 July, 28 October 1897; *Weekly Sun*, 13 August 1897, 6 May, 6 December 1898; *The Times*, 25 October 1897; *Liverpool Mercury* (a particularly enthusiastic supporter of the NPRA), 15 April, 2 October, 17 December 1897, 23 August 1899, 1 March 1900. The palaeographer Sir Edward Maunde Thompson was director of the British Museum. Stone's photograph of a Wyre Forest charcoal burner was awarded third prize in a competition organised by the *Graphic*, 3 April 1897.

[23] Edwards, James and Barnes, *A Record of England*, pp. 16-17.

band' and placed in the stocks; in September 1903 a dummy funeral had been arranged for him in Aberdeen with the bearers of the coffin wearing traditional dress. He estimated that by 1905 he had used three tons of glass in photographic plates. During these years there were a number of exhibitions of the NPRA's work in London, in provincial cities, including Birmingham, and at the St. Louis World Fair (where Stone exhibited 300 photographs). 'I consider that you are', his friend the Byzantine historian Sir Edwin Pears (1835-1919) informed him at this highpoint of the NPRA's activities, 'one of the most valuable historians of the time. When number of volumes written by myself and great chroniclers have ceased to exist, your collection will be again and again reproduced...'[24]

* * * *

Stone voted loyally for the Unionist administrations of Salisbury and, after July 1902, of Balfour in the House of Commons. In his utterances at constituency party meetings, he defended the 'concentration camps' in South Africa, into which Boer women and children were gathered, on the grounds that they were protected against famine and under proper supervision. Stone was a party man, but privately he must have second thoughts when the horrifyingly high death rates from malnutrition and disease in these camps were reported. He also made clear his firm support for Education Act (1902) and the Aliens Act (1905), declaring that extending the provision of secondary education and limiting immigration from Eastern Europe could only benefit the people of East Birmingham.

Undoubtedly Stone left himself wide open to attack from his opponents. It could not be denied that he had been far more interested in taking pictures on the terrace than in making speeches in the chamber. The Liberal *Birmingham Argus* was relentless – and often very amusing – in its coverage of Stone's apparent

---

[24] *The Times*, 9 March 1900; *Western Gazette*, 10 May 1901; *Gloucester Citizen*, 22 May 1902; *Dundee Courier*, 23 September 1903; *Aberdeen Journal*, 26 February 1904; *Manchester Courier*, 17 November 1905; Library of Birmingham, 150 Stray Letters, Pears to Stone, 19 September 1903.

lethargy. 'He is not in a far country nor asleep in the lobby', the paper observed when Stone met his constituency officers at the House of Commons, 'Presumably ... [they] were anxious to know whether their member was still in the land of the living and could be convinced of the fact by optical demonstration'. If Stone was relieved when this newspaper ceased publication in June 1902, he soon found himself under fire from a Labour candidate in his own constituency.

James Holmes resumed the attack on Stone's low profile, declaring that, in 1904, he had voted in only forty of every 100 divisions in the House of Commons and had not made a single speech there or in his constituency. James Holmes (1861-1934) was a full time organiser for the Amalgamated Society of Railway Servants. Brought up by his mother in rural poverty in Lincolnshire, he had long believed that working men should be elected to the House of Commons and proposed the resolution at the 1899 TUC that had led to the formation of the Labour Representative Committee, subsequently the Labour Party. He had also been prominently involved in the Taff Vale case of 1901, which made trade unions financially liable for losses sustained by their employers during industrial disputes. In a constituency full of railway workers Holmes was an ideal candidate, and, for him, Stone, an employer, was an ideal opponent. When he was informed of Holmes' adoption as a candidate in June 1903, Stone must have looked at this political bruiser who had a talent for public speaking and understood that he faced the political fight of his life.

It was not only a confirmed challenge in East Birmingham that gave Stone cause for concern in the summer of 1903. Chamberlain, in a dramatic speech at Bingley Hall in Birmingham in May, had come out against free trade and in favour of closer economic ties across the Empire. The result of Chamberlain's declaration was a split in the Unionist ranks between free traders and tariff reformers. Balfour sought wriggle room for himself by urging some retaliation against foreign tariffs where necessary. Stone, had to make his mind up where he stood on this matter, and, in October 1903, announced that 'they would be unwise in binding themselves any stronger to the fiscal programme than the Prime Minister had gone'. It was a position Stone soon moved away from, doubtless pressurized by Chamberlain to come into line. 'I can imagine the eyeglass looking at him', Holmes observed, 'and the great man saying, "Benjamin, I am afraid you are beyond hope and, unless you become a whole hogger, I shall not come and adorn the Carlton Theatre", and Sir Benjamin would say, "Joseph, you have always thought for me, think again"'. Stone shrugged off such attacks: all that mattered was that he, Chamberlain and Balfour supported some form of fiscal change and Holmes, the LRC and the Liberals did not.

Speaking regularly in East Birmingham, Holmes certainly became a thorn in Stone's side. He defended free trade and called for the nationalisation of the railways, but always sought to keep his sights on Stone, whom he accused of torpidity and of being Chamberlain's stooge. Furiously assailed by the local Chamberlainite press, Holmes did manage to secure the support of the Saltley vicar James Adderley, who gave 'splendid help in the fight'. For his part Stone, both in the run-up to the election and during the campaign itself in January 1906, stuck firmly to Chamberlain's line. Tariff reform, he argued, offered the only solution to unemployment. He was specific in his speeches, declaring that the Metropolitan Amalgamated Railway Company, a large employer in his constituency, was threatened by the importation of railway carriages from America. Chamberlain himself arrived - his only appearance in the city outside his own constituency - to bolster support for Stone. 'I am going back to Parliament, if I go at all, in favour of tariff reform ...', a revitalised Stone declared.[25]

Heckled at meetings and with Unionist seats falling in the north, Stone privately expected defeat. 'Railwaymen are voting in shoals for James Holmes', it was reported on polling day, 'and Sir Benjamin Stone's dismissal is regarded as already assured.' But by a majority of only 585 votes, he was returned. He was assured by one of his own canvassers that 'a great majority of poor people have a very warm and affectionate regard for you and I would say it was your personality which carried you to the head of the poll'. The socialist vicar James Adderley saw matters differently. 'The worship of Mr Chamberlain is quite extraordinary', he wrote a few weeks later. 'I had thought there was some exaggeration about this. There is none'. Stone, though almost sixty eight years old, could have stood aside but, unpalatable as it was, had been determined to take

---

[25] *BDG*, 12 January 1906; *Manchester Guardian*, 15 January 1906.

on Holmes. For him the election result was a vindication of an ideology that had guided him from the outset of his political career—that the working man was a natural Conservative.[26]

---

[26] The *Star*, 17 January 1906; Library of Birmingham, 150 Stray Letters, W.H. Bailey to Stone, 2 February 1906.

8 The Fear of the Future

With his garage for two motor cars at The Grange, his telephone, his vacuum cleaners and, of course, his cameras, Stone seemed to have embraced modernity. When, in September 1909, Louis Bleriot visited London, it was Stone who gave him lunch at the House of Commons, declaring that aviation would lead to 'great results ... not only in military, but also scientific, matters'. Stone recognised that his world was changing, but there were changes about which he was uneasy, even alarmed. These were principally in the political sphere. The Liberal Government elected in 1906 became increasingly radical on constitutional issues. In 1909-11 Stone feared the emasculation of the House of Lords and Home Rule for Ireland. 'Do you seek to return to Parliament again?' the geologist Henry Woodward enquired with great pessimism in December 1909. 'Or are you tired of the present administration and its Radico-Socialist, Home Rule, down-with-everything programme?' At the lunch given to mark Stone's retirement from the House of Commons in November 1909, his fellow MP Sidney Buxton quipped that 'they would be glad of his records of the House of Lords when, perhaps in a year or two, it had ceased to exist'. This mildly humorous remark contained more than a grain of truth for men like Stone. He certainly agreed with the sentiments expressed in a letter from his old friend Henry Matthews that 'the House of Commons becomes less attractive for quiet, reasonable men'. 'Labour men much in evidence', Stone recorded more than once in his parliamentary diaries in these years. These Labour men talked of socialism, a word Stone almost spat out. Politically, this normally optimistic man feared the worst.[1]

At The Grange life carried on much as it always had. Five of Stone's six children were married by the time of his seventieth

---

[1] *Western Times,* 16 September 1909; Library of Birmingham, 150 Stray Letters, Woodward to Stone, 31 December 1909, Matthews to Stone, 26 December 1909; The Parliamentary Diaries of Sir J. B. Stone, 3 November 1906; *The Times*, 5 November 1909. At the lunch held in his honour, a selection of the photographs Stone had taken of MPs and the Houses of Parliament were displayed, and these, rather than his political fears, formed the subject matter of his speech.

birthday: Ethel was married to a Walsall leather manufacturer Robert Holden and Dora to a London doctor Daniel McKenzie (who later became a leading throat and ear specialist) whilst Norman (the owner of a cosmetics business), Oscar and Roland (a publisher) lived with their wives in Brentford, Sutton Coldfield and Hampstead respectively. Family gatherings were soon enlivened by the presence of a large number of grandchildren. Only Barron remained at home and was not to marry until 1920. Over dinner Stone would hear from Barron and Oscar about their awkward relations with the Smiths at the paper mills; Stone was horrified when, in March 1908, Parker Smith put himself forward as a candidate for Erdington council. Jane, meanwhile, continued to call on friends in the area and hold functions at the house. In March 1907, she invited a speaker to address thirty-two ladies from the Erdington Shakespearean Society and in February 1909, organised a whist party. With Ethel and her family, she enjoyed holidays in Llandudno. There was 'a merry party', attended by fifty people, in the grounds of The Grange in September 1907 to mark the hundredth birthday of Stone's mother. By this time James Stone was showing the signs of old age. 'Found him feeble but clear-headed & wishful to be pleasant & chatty', Stone noted in his diary. 'Clara reports him to be very uncertain'. His brother died in mid-December 1908 'after slight sickness, Clara holding his head at the moment of his attempting to vomit'. When Stone received this news, he was also very concerned about Jane, who had recently hurt herself in two falls. [2]

There was solace to be found from his political fears and personal worries in photography and travel. Stone spent the winter of 1906-1907 with fellow photographer John Brigg in Egypt, having planned the expedition through Cook & Sons. He had hoped to see the long-serving consul-general Lord Cromer, but the meeting was cancelled and so instead Stone enjoyed 'an exceedingly pleasant interview' with the Khedive. During this tour Stone took 800 photographs, including 'many views of mosques', pilgrims, fishermen, school children and, amongst other historic sites, the

---

[2] Library of Birmingham, The Parliamentary Diaries of Sir J. B. Stone, 15 March, 4 September, 30 September 1907, 6 April, 19 November, 1 December, 16 December 1908. Clara was James Stone's unmarried daughter, born in 1855.

tombs at Deir el Bahri on the west bank of the Nile where he found the archaeologist Edouard Naville at work. Ever ingenious, he hired a troupe of dancers 'to overcome the shyness of the Bisharin villagers...whom he photographed as they watched the dancing'. Stone was to spend an entire week labelling his pictures on his return for display at a conversazione at the Royal Society. 'My exhibition of Egyptian photographs was very popular', he noted with great pleasure in his diary. 'The general greeting was "I have seen your beautiful photographs'. In May 1907, Stone was engrossed in photographic work at the British Museum and the Natural History Museum, and he also visited the office of the *Photographic Journal* 'to see the collection of Record Photographs (mostly mine) ... on view'. In July 1907, he was invited to spend the weekend at Bear Wood, owned by the proprietor of *The Times* Arthur Walter. 'A fine estate of 7000 acres & a modern mansion of great grandeur', he recorded. 'I photographed the house and grounds ...' [3]

In taking these photographs and developing them, Stone was assisted as ever by Mercer. When Mercer broke his ribs in an accident in early 1908, Stone's photographic exploits were somewhat curtailed. In the spring of that year Stone spent a month in Turkey, but was disappointed on his return when he called on Mercer to inspect his photographs. 'He made an excuse that his wife's business had detained him in Exeter & therefore no work had been done in my absence, though I sent him heavy boxes by Mr Frew ...' Stone was 'well-satisfied' when he saw the photographs, and took his camera with him when he visited the south of France that autumn. Always well prepared for his expeditions, he compiled a list of eighty three essential items to be taken, including eighteen handkerchiefs, two candles, his eye glass, his teeth box, his umbrella, a hammer, a corkscrew, lozenges and medicine for diarrhoea.[4] His medicines did not prevent him from feeling unwell on reaching home. 'Still feeling poorly after my journey', he wrote a few days after his return. 'Meals in railway carriages and French

---

[3] S. Roberts, 'The Photographer-MP', p. 36; Library of Birmingham, Sir J. B. Stone Newspaper Cuttings, 5, p. 37; Library of Birmingham, Parliamentary Diaries of Sir J. B. Stone, 9 May 1907; *BDP,* 17 May 1907
[4] Jay, *Customs & Faces,* n.p.

wines have upset me'. [5] Stone's final ventures abroad took him 'on a tour of inspection of Moorish antiquities in the old cities of Spain' in spring 1910 and to Turkey and Egypt in the winter of 1909-1910.[6] Though now in his early seventies, Stone would have carried on with his travels had it not been for the ill-health that beset Jane. By 1911, he was employing a live-in nurse to care for Jane, who was suffering from cancer and had endured both operations and radium treatment.

The NPRA was wound up in May 1910. At the final meeting of the organisation Stone took a swipe at picture postcards, 'the cheap representation of things', they had 'prevented the development of good photography'. Fewer photographers than Stone had hoped had become involved in the NPRA, put off by the annual membership fee of ten shillings or by the regulations on how photographs should be taken and developed. Whilst some areas of the country, particularly where Stone was active, were well-covered, others yielded few rewards. So there were hundreds of photographs of Warwickshire but less than a dozen of Devon. In total 5,883 photographs were assembled, 1532 by Stone himself. He was the chief contributor to the work of the NPRA. It would perhaps be unfair to describe the NPRA as a personal vanity project for Stone. Indeed Edwards, James and Barnes suggest that, for all its shortcomings, it should be seen as a memorial to Stone's own imagination and creativity.[7] The publicity which the NPRA gave record photography certainly inspired some amateurs, and it was replaced by the less centralised Federation of Photographic Record and Survey Societies. Stone, naturally enough, became president.

In these last years, Stone photographic career reached what he regarded as its zenith. His photographs of the procession of Edward VIII through London in October 1902 had been greatly admired. In April 1911 he was informed–probably after some discreet lobbying on his behalf - that he was to be the official photographer for the coronation of George V. Stone intended to take photographs of both the procession and the crowning itself. A

---

[5] Library of Birmingham, 'The Parliamentary Diaries of Sir J. B. Stone', 19 May, 3 October, 6 October 1908.
[6] *Evening Telegraph,* 20 April 1910.
[7] *Cheltenham Chronicle,* 4 June 1910; Edwards, James and Barnes, (eds.), *A Record of England,* p. 24.

room was fitted up for his use in Westminster Abbey, and, as 22 June approached, his excitement grew. Unfortunately on coronation day he was unwell, and it was his son Roland who took the photographs. Stone had always been aware of the dimness of the light of Westminster Abbey, and was not able to use flashes. These lighting difficulties were not satisfactorily overcome, and the photographs were dark. *The Times*, in its account of the day's events, did not even mention Stone's photographic activities. He also knew that he had been eclipsed by a more exciting new technology - Pathe News had made a short film of the procession. Stone's world was, indeed, changing. [8]

The Liberal election landslide - and the return for the first time of a large number of Labour MPs - in 1906 filled Stone with unease. For Stone things got off to a bad start and then got progressively worse. He objected, in autumn 1906, to the Agricultural Holdings Bill, which provided compensation to tenants for improvements. This mild measure was 'outrageous ... but, with the Government majority, we are helpless'. He described the use of the guillotine to get the Scottish Land Bill through the House of Commons in early 1908 as 'disgraceful'. When the Liberals resorted later that year to the same tactics to assist the Old Age Pensions Bill and then the Licensing Bill, Stone was indignant. 'A ridiculous absurdity to call it a debate', he wrote on one occasion. Apart from the denial of debate, Stone disapproved of the content of these Bills. He was impressed by the dogged resistance to old age pensions of the maverick Liberal MP Harold Cox, and saw in the licensing proposals nothing but 'injustice & confiscation'. [9]

And then there were the Labour MPs. 'Socialists rampant ...', 'The usual Labour grumbling ...' he reported on two occasions in summer 1908. These men represented 'the dangerous wave of socialism', which Stone had, rather alarmingly, also observed in East Birmingham. It was his opinion that the socialist vicar of Saltley James Adderley, who had supported the Labour candidate Holmes in 1906, 'talked platitudes about the poor, nothing instructive or

---

[8] *The Times*, 6 April 1911.
[9] Roberts, 'The Photographer-MP', pp. 36-7. All quotations in this and the following paragraph are from this essay. See, Library of Birmingham, Sir J. B. Stone Newspaper Cuttings, 5, p. 42, for Stone's hostility to the Liberal reforms.

useful'. At a meeting with his constituency officers in the smoking room of the House of Commons in February 1908, Stone 'made it plain that if I did not get assistance, I should not carry on a campaign against socialism or contest the next election'. Now seventy Stone was losing heart for the fight. Taking stock of it all, the man who had taken on the all-conquering Birmingham Liberals thirty years earlier could only conclude that the situation was 'gloomy'. He decided that he would not seek re-election. He became, during his final year in the House of Commons, an absentee MP. [10]

From The Grange Stone watched with horror as the Liberals launched their assault on the House of Lords in 1910-11. The Unionists had used their majority in the Lords to weaken or destroy Liberal legislation, culminating in the rejection of the 'People's Budget' in November 1909. For Stone it was doing its job–the House of Lords was there to curtail the ambitions of dangerous governments. Now the constitution itself was to be turned upside down. He also had not one iota of sympathy for the Suffragettes: having heard Christabel Pankhurst 'wildly talking from a cart' in Bury St. Edmunds in August 1908, he was sure that women were too excitable to have a say in law-making. Stone, and the circle of friends with whom he corresponded, really did feel like men out of time. 'Our Radical Government have upset the constitution', Matthews informed him at the end of 1911, 'abolished the House of Lords, gagged and degraded the House of Commons and lit the flame of labour unrest of which we see only the beginning. None of us can say what the end will be'. [11]

In February 1912, Stone informed an old friend of his 'sadness in passing the milestones towards the end of life's journey'. That year came the shock of the death of his seventeen year old grandson Edward Holden in a climbing accident in the Alps. He had strayed

---

[10] *Exeter and Plymouth Gazette,* 23 October 1909.
[11] Roberts, 'The Photographer-MP', p. 36; Library of Birmingham, 150 Stray Letters, Matthews to Stone, 31 December 1911. *Tamworth Herald,* 19 November 1910, for Stone's attendance at a dinner in Sutton Coldfield at which F. A. Newdegate, the MP for Tamworth defended the House of Lords.

from his party to pick wild flowers.[12] There were also the deaths of friends to cope with, including Henry Matthews, afflicted with severe rheumatism in his final years, in April 1913. With Jane bed-ridden, Stone spent most of his time at The Grange. Once he and Jane had accepted most of the invitations to attend functions they had received, but now Stone went alone or not at all on account of his own 'indifferent health'. It was suggested to him by friends that he write his autobiography, but he did not feel he had the stamina for that. Someone else would tell his story he was sure, and so he prepared the material for his future biographer. He organised his massive scrapbooks – he had employed a press cuttings agency at the height of his fame in the late 1890s and early 1900s – sorted through his letters and re-wrote his parliamentary diaries. He stipulated that he did not want his collections separated after his death, but did not make any arrangements for depositing them anywhere. In May 1913, there was a final exhibition of Stone's photographs in Birmingham. That autumn he entertained a party of geologists in Sutton Coldfield. By this stage he was afflicted by recurring bouts of ill health.[13]

What was it like to have been John Benjamin Stone? It had, for the most part, been a contented life. It was only in his final decade that he experienced any real anxieties. He was unnerved by the growing popularity of socialist ideas, dismayed by the constitutional changes ushered in by the Liberals, irritated by the attitude of his main business partner at the paper mills and upset by the ill health of his half-brother and his wife. Politically, Stone was never truly a democrat. He believed that working people were best represented by men like himself who knew their interests and not by their own class; and he defended the right of an unelected House of Lords to block the legislation of an elected House of Commons. A family man and a builder of enduring friendships is certainly what Stone was, and these secure ties helped make him the placid, genial man at ease with his world that he was presented as in the newspapers. From his early years in business, Stone made more

---

[12] Library of Birmingham, Copies of Illuminated and Other Addresses, Stone to C. F. Marston, 11 February 1912; *Lichfield Mercury,* 16 February, 30 August 1912. *Tamworth Herald,* 19 July 1912, *Express and Star,* 27 August 1912, for the death of Edward Holden.
[13] *Dundee Courier,* 1 November 1909.

than enough money to enable him to do the things he wanted to do. He spent lavishly on travel and photography. He was a buoyant man at all stages of his life, enjoying enormously, for example, the full page cartoon depictions of him in satirical magazine the *Dart* - but perhaps the happiest time of all in his life was his first decade in Parliament. He became, after 1895, a household name, an amiable, rotund, bewhiskered, unfashionably-dressed photographer-MP, welcome almost everywhere he wanted to go with his camera.

In early 1878, the enterprising business Cigar Divan of Prince's Corner, New Street, Birmingham had produced an advertisement featuring Stone asking Chamberlain where he had got 'that beautiful cigar'. It was a question that Stone, affable as he was, probably did not put to Chamberlain in 1878; but after 1886, at dinner parties at Highbury, the question may well have come up.[14] If Stone lacked the aloofness and vanity of Chamberlain, he shared with him a determination to get the outcomes he wanted. In early 1914 these two one-time adversaries who later formed a firm political alliance were nearing the end of their lives. Stone had been reported to be 'seriously unwell' in January, but had managed to celebrate his seventy-sixth birthday the following month. Chamberlain, paralysed by a stroke in July 1906, suffered a heart attack in May. At The Grange on 8.30pm on 2 July 1914, Stone died; Jane following him three days later. One hundred miles away in London, less than two hours after Stone's death, Chamberlain met his end.[15]

---

[14] University of Birmingham, Joseph Chamberlain Papers, C/4/11-12, records Stone dining at Highbury on 25 January 1889, 26 January 1892 and 2 October 1899.
[15] Library of Birmingham, Sir J. B. Stone Newspaper Cuttings, 23; *Manchester Courier,* 8 January 1914; *BDP,* 3 July, 8 July 1914; *Erdington News*, 11 July 1914; *Tamworth Herald,* 11 July 1914.

Photographs

The first photograph Stone bought - in Bergen, Norway, 1864.

The Grange, Stone's house in Birmingham, 1897

The library at The Grange, where Stone spent much of his time when he was at home, 1896

The showroom at Stone, Fawdry, Stone Union Glassworks, 1890

The bag room at Smith, Stone & Knight Paper Mills, 1895

The Vesey Club, with Stone bottom right, in Norway, 1890

Stone, on the right, and companion in Japan, 1891

Women and children in Bisharin in Egypt, 1907

Henry Matthews addressing an election meeting in East Birmingham, 1892

MPs sitting in the House of Commons, 1903

Joseph Chamberlain on the terrace of the House of Commons, 1902

Stone on the terrace of the House of Commons, 1905

Louis Bleriot and his wife on the terrace of the House of Commons, 1909

Floral Tributes on the Day of the Funeral of Queen Victoria, 1901

Stone in the stocks at the pole fair in Corby, Northamptonshire, 1902

Maypole dancing in Sherborne, Dorset, 1907

Gypsy encampment, Blackpool, 1906

Rock houses in Kinver, Worcestershire, 1897

Boys in classroom at Josiah Mason Orphanage, Birmingham, 1908

Colmore Row, from St Philip's churchyard, Birmingham, 1910

Bibliographical Note

Sir Benjamin Stone was a man who seemingly never threw anything away. There is, in the Library of Birmingham, an enormous amount of material relating to him, deposited by his eldest son Barron in July 1919. The most well-known part of the collection is, of course, the photographs - 22,000 mounted prints and 17,000 glass negatives. But there are also many scrapbooks – at my last count almost forty - containing newspaper cuttings and political and business memorabilia as well as volumes of letters, cards, addresses and parliamentary diaries. I cannot emphasise enough what a treasure trove these volumes of newspaper cuttings and memorabilia are – they contain, unbeknownst to many scholars of Victorian politics, letters from leading statesmen, tickets for meetings, reports, cartoons and posters. They deserve to be mined not so much by those interested in Stone but by those interested in the Conservative cause in the second half of the nineteenth century. Neatly-written letters from Sir Stafford Northcote, an ink sketch by Jesse Collings, cartoons from the satirical magazines of Birmingham, posters from the general election of 1880, leaflets and tickets for the great Conservative demonstration in Aston Park in 1884, police notices for the day of Gladstone's funeral, tickets for the coronation of Edward VII, three line whips 'most earnestly' requesting the presence of Unionist MPs in the House of Commons ... these, and much more, can be found in these fascinating volumes.

Over thirty years ago I was able to examine material that had remained in the possession of the Stone family. This collection was then in the possession of Stone's grand daughter Jane Brooker. It is a not inconsiderable collection, including photographs, a family scrapbook, family correspondence between 1879 and 1884, a volume of letters Stone sent home as he travelled around the world in 1891 and a notebook from 1908. At the time of writing, I have been unable to establish where this material is now located.

It is very likely that a biography of Stone would have been published soon after his death had this not occurred on the eve of the outbreak of the First World War. In the post-war years Stone, the archetypal Victorian, seemed to very definitely belong to a different age. Bill Jay began the attempts to recover the story of Stone's life. Though the introduction to his *Customs and Faces: The Photographs of Sir Benjamin Stone* (1972) does contain gaps, it is not without interest. For many years now the custodian of Stone's legacy has been Peter James. His published work on Stone's photographic work is excellent. I have found his essay 'Evolution of the Photographic Record and Survey Movement c. 1890-1910' in *England: Sir Benjamin Stone & the National Photographic Record Association 1897-1910* (2006), co-edited with Elizabeth Edwards and Martin Barnes, most helpful. In writing about Stone's political activities I have been on firmer ground, but for reminding myself about the issues of the day it has been reassuring to have been able to call on: Ian Cawood, *The Liberal Unionist Party: A History* (2012); Peter Marsh, *Joseph Chamberlain: Entrepreneur in Politics* (1994); Robert Rhodes James, *The British Revolution: British Politics 1880-1939* (1976), G. R. Searle, *A New England? Peace and War 1886-1918* (Oxford, 2006); and Roger Ward, *City-State and Nation: Birmingham's Political History 1830-1940* (Chichester, 2005).

Index

About the Author

Stephen Roberts is Visiting Research Fellow in Victorian History at Newman University, Birmingham. His interest in Victorian and Edwardian Birmingham is long-standing, and has resulted in essays and reviews in the *Birmingham Historian*, *West Midlands Studies* and *Midland History* as well as a short biography of the antiquarian and poet John Alfred Langford (1823-1903). The author of a number of books on Chartism, he periodically talks about this subject on BBC Radio 3 and BBC Radio 4.

29577629R00064

Made in the USA
Charleston, SC
17 May 2014